HTML 4

in easy steps

"CECEEF." smokey 1.Pac

M.Barge

MIKE MCGRATH

COMPUTER STEP

In easy steps is an imprint of Computer Step
Southfield Road . Southam
Warwickshire CV47 OFB . England

http://www.ineasysteps.com

Notice of Liability
Every effort has been made to ensure that this book contains accurate
and current information. However, Computer Step and the author shall
not be liable for any loss or damage suffered by readers as a result of
any information contained herein.

Trademarks
All trademarks are acknowledged as belonging to their respective
companies.

Printed and bound in the United Kingdom

ISBN 1-84078-048-7

Table Of Contents

Introducing HTML 4

Welcome to the world of HTML 4 – the latest standard for the creation of Internet pages.

This chapter introduces the Hypertext Markup Language (HTML) with a brief history and examines how HTML fits into the World Wide Web. There is a discussion of HTML authoring tools and a demonstration of Web page structure.

Covers

Chapter One

History of HTML

Historically, the desire to have text printed in specific formats meant that original manuscripts had to be "marked up" with annotation to indicate to the book-printer how sections of text should be laid out.

W3C is the recognised body that oversees standards on the Web. See the latest developments on their informative Web site at http://www.w3c.org.

This annotation had to be concise and needed to be understood both by the printer and the text originator.

A series of commonly recognised abbreviations therefore formed the basis of a markup "language".

HTML is a modern markup language that uses common abbreviations called "tags" to advise a Web browser how the author would like to have the Web page displayed.

It was devised in the late 1980s by a British scientist named Tim Berners-Lee while he was working at the Particle Physics laboratory in Cern, Switzerland.

The simplicity of HTML led it to become popular in the early days of the Internet with text-based Web browsers.

A major development with HTML came in 1993 when a college student named Marc Anderssen added an image tag so that HTML could display images in addition to text.

The current version of Microsoft Internet Explorer is based on the Mosaic browser from NCSA.

This version was then included in the Mosaic Web browser from the National Center for Supercomputing Applications (NCSA) and became very successful.

Marc went on to establish the Netscape Web browser.

By the mid 1990s various Web browsers that were fighting for market share began to add proprietary tags to effectively create their own versions of HTML.

The World Wide Web Consortium (W3C) recognised the danger that HTML could become fragmented and acted to create a standard to which all Web browsers should adhere.

Today Tim Berners-Lee is a director of the W3C and the latest version of the W3C HTML standard is the HTML 4.01 recommendation that is used throughout this book.

What's New in HTML 4

The features in the earlier standard of HTML 3.2 have been updated in HTML 4 to provide more flexibility for current and future development of the Internet.

The style sheet examples given in this book use specifications of version CSS2.0.

HTML 4 separates the presentational markup tags from the actual content with the introduction of Cascading Style Sheets (CSS) that are used to control how content appears.

This is the single biggest change in HTML 4 but there are many other significant changes.

All tags are still contained between the "<" and ">" angle brackets but many of the earlier tags have become obsolete.

The old "<center>" tag is no longer used to centre text on the page nor is the "<font>" tag now used to control the selection of a font style for a piece of text.

Instead a style sheet controls these presentational details.

The range of available style sheet properties gives much greater possibilities in how the content may be displayed.

New tags have been added to extend the precision of how HTML may define the document content.

To increase the global utilisation of HTML, support has been added for languages that are written from right to left.

A new model is introduced for the layout of tables that allow a browser to start rendering a table even before the entire table has been downloaded.

Greater scripting possibilities have been created by the addition of more page "events" that react to the user.

HTML 4 has been designed to make Web pages more accessible to those with physical limitations.

Exciting possibilities are presented with the inclusion of further new tags for the creation of compound Web documents. These allow multiple documents from a variety of sources to be combined into a single Web page.

Addressing Web Pages

The really special component of HTML is the hypertext link that allows the user to easily navigate around the Internet.

In order for this to be possible the Internet must use established standards for all computers which are connected to the World Wide Web.

The Web comprises a series of large computers, referred to as "servers", that are connected via telephone and satellite. Connecting any computer by telephone to any one of these servers can provide access to all files across the Web.

The Web uses a common communication standard called HyperText Transfer Protocol (HTTP) to allow instant communication between all computers and Web servers.

This common protocol permits the Web browser to retrieve Web pages from any part of the Web and is always used as the first part of a Web page address, expressed as "http://".

It is necessary for each Web document to have a unique address so that the user can locate a specific document. In the same way that a postal address may be a combination of city name, street name and addressee name, a Web address combines protocol name, domain name and file name.

HTML files are merely text files that have been saved with a file extension of either ".htm" or ".html" so a typical index Web page could have a file name of "index.html".

A Web page address should not contain any spaces.

If this page was uploaded to a Web server that has the domain name "www.webserver" then the page would be accessible across the Web using the Web page address of http://www.webserver/index.html.

Usually, uploaded files are placed in a folder on the server so its Web page address would include the folder name:

Protocol	Domain	File Name
http://	www.webserver/subfolder/	index.html

Absolute and Relative Addresses

The full address of a Web page, using the protocol, domain and file name, is called the "absolute" address.

Below is an illustration of a folder on a Web server that has the domain name "www.webserver".

The index Web page can be addressed with its absolute address of "http://www.webserver/webpages/index.html".

If in doubt always use the full absolute address to avoid confusion.

HTML code in the "index.html" file can also address any files within the "webpages" folder just using their file name.

This is called the "relative" address.

In the illustration, code in "index.html" file can refer to the "next.html" file simply as "next.html", or with the absolute address of "http://www.webserver/webpages/next.html".

A relative address can also refer to a file within the upper level folder that contains the current folder by preceding its file name with the syntax " ../ ".

In the illustration, any document in the "extra" folder could address the "next.html" document in the "webpages" folder as "../next.html".

Alternatively the absolute address can also be used to address the "next.html" document from within any other document as "http://www.webserver/webpages/next.html".

Fragment Addresses

Navigating to either an absolute or relative address will normally open that document at the start of the page.

It is possible however to add navigation points to the HTML code inside a Web page to allow quick navigation to specific points in that page.

See chapter 7 on "Hyperlinks And Anchors" for more info and examples.

These navigation points are called "anchors" and are always given a name by which they can be addressed.

In the example on the previous page the file named "next.html" has fragment anchors at the start, middle and end of the document.

These anchors are called "top", "middle" and "bottom".

This page can be opened in a Web browser at a specific point in the document by adding the required anchor name to the end of the page address.

These added anchor names are referred to as "fragment identifiers" and must be preceded by a "#" character.

The address to open "next.html" at the middle anchor is "http://www.webserver/webpages/next.html#middle".

If addressing this page and anchor from another file in the same folder the relative address "next.html#middle" could be used to open the document at the middle anchor.

Document Type Definitions

The first line of a valid HTML document should contain a declaration of the version of HTML used in that document.

This declaration is called a "Document Type Definition", or commonly just "DTD" for short.

The DTD is just a piece of code, specified in the HTML standard, that can be pasted into the top of each page.

It states the Web page address containing the language rules for that version of HTML.

 The Web browser can use the address in the DTD to validate the HTML code contained in that document.

All code given in this book is to the W3C HTML 4.01 specifications that offers three DTDs that can be used.

The standard DTD is called "Strict" and should be used for a HTML document that only uses valid HTML 4 markup:

```
<!DOCTYPE HTML PUBLIC "-//W3C//DTD HTML 4.01//EN"
          "http://www.w3.org/TR/html4/strict.dtd">
```

The specification also provides a "Transitional" DTD for backwards compatibility. This should be used where the HTML document contains some older markup that has become obsolete in the HTML 4 strict standard:

```
<!DOCTYPE HTML PUBLIC
"-//W3C//DTD HTML 4.01 Transitional//EN"
"http://www.w3.org/TR/html4/loose.dtd">
```

Finally there is a special DTD that is only to be used for a HTML "frameset" document that specifies the frames to be used in a multi-document Web page:

```
<!DOCTYPE HTML PUBLIC
"-//W3C//DTD HTML 4.01 Frameset//EN"
"http://www.w3.org/TR/html4/frameset.dtd">
```

As the example code given in this book does not use any obsolete markup the Strict DTD will be used in all HTML documents except the frameset examples in chapter 9.

HTML Document Structure

A HTML 4 document is comprised of these three parts:

1. A Document Type Definition (DTD).

2. A Head section containing document information.

3. A Body section containing the actual content.

The DTD should appear at the top of the document to declare the HTML version being used in the document.

This is followed by a HTML <head> tag denoting the start of the Head section and a </head> tag to mark its end.

HTML tags are mostly used in this way as "containers" with the syntax < [tag name] > </ [tag name] >.

The HTML <head> </head> tags contain the Head section information of a HTML document.

Similarly the HTML <body> </body> tags are used to contain the actual content of the HTML document.

The example below illustrates the three parts that comprise all HTML 4 documents:

Develop the habit now of using lowercase characters for HTML tags.

```
<!DOCTYPE HTML PUBLIC "-//W3C//DTD HTML 4.01//EN"
          "http://www.w3.org/TR/html4/strict.dtd">

<head>

    [ The document information code goes here ]

</head>

<body>

    [ The actual document content goes here ]

</body>
```

The HTML 4 tag names may use uppercase or lowercase characters. Future versions may allow only lowercase however so lowercase is used throughout this book.

Hello World

The head section of a document should always contain exactly one set of <title> tags. These are used to set the document title that is usually seen in the window title bar.

The example below adds a title in the Head section and simple text inside <p> paragraph tags in the Body section:

 The old <html> tags that were used to enclose all the Html code are no longer required to be used.

```
<!DOCTYPE HTML PUBLIC "-//W3C//DTD HTML 4.01//EN"
          "http://www.w3.org/TR/html4/strict.dtd">
<head>
<title>Greetings</title>
</head>

<body>
<!-- The Traditional Start -->
<p>Hello World</p>
</body>
```

Hello World

 The "invisible" characters that represent tabs, new lines, carriage returns and spaces are collectively known as "whitespace".

Notice that the code in the body section also contains a HTML comment that is not displayed by the browser.

Any text that appears between the special comment identifiers "<!--" and "-->" are ignored by the browser.

This applies both to single-line comments and comments that are spread over many lines.

The Web browser also ignores the "invisible characters" that represent tabs, new lines, and carriage returns.

Multiple spaces are commuted to just a single space. This means that the browser output in the example above would remain the same even if the code left multiple spaces between the two content words.

HTML Tools

HTML code can be created in any basic text editor and does not require any special software.

In fact, many professional HTML writers use the simple Notepad application included with Microsoft Windows.

As long as the code in the new text file is saved with a file extension of either ".htm" or ".html" a HTML file is made.

This file can then be opened in any recent version of Microsoft Internet Explorer to see the browser output.

Some Netscape browsers and other older browsers may not fully recognize the HTML 4 specifications.

It is best therefore to run HTML 4 Web pages in a modern version of Internet Explorer. This browser is also by far the most popular Web browser used on the Internet.

To validate the HTML code written in a finished document it is best to avoid the proprietary validator applications that are available which may not fully meet the standards.

The W3C have a free on-line validation service that will quickly validate the code of any HTML 4 document.

If the HTML document is located on the Web the W3C HTML validator at "http://validator.w3.org" can be used for an instant validation.

If the document is just on the local computer, say on the desktop, use "http://validator.w3.org/file-upload.html" where the W3C validator will quickly upload the file then return instant validation results.

The validator has useful options and gives helpful output.

To encourage correct HTML code to be used on the Internet the W3C validator offers a verification image with correct validation results.

This can prove useful to Web developers to assure their clients that the code which they are supplying has been tested to the correct standards.

Microsoft FrontPage

The FrontPage application from Microsoft is one of the most successful of the so-called "WYSIWYG" HTML editors (What-You-See-Is-What-You-Get).

FrontPage and similar HTML editors can be used to create and quickly test handwritten HTML 4 code.

They all offer the advantages of colour highlighting of the HTML tags and other syntax when viewing the HTML code.

Also all have a quick and easy way to preview code under development that simulates its output in a Web browser.

FrontPage has tabs at the bottom of the window to toggle views between the code and preview windows.

FrontPage does not make real validation checks on the HTML code and may appear to correctly preview bad code.

HTML Authoring Tips

The W3C HTML 4.01 specification makes these general recommendations to Web page authors:

1. Separate structure and presentation

As the Internet develops, a wider range of devices are expected to access HTML documents on a variety of platforms (cellphones, PDAs, etc.).

It is therefore recommended that the Web page author should now use style sheets for all presentational aspects of a HTML document.

This enables one document to be more easily readable across a wide range of devices and platforms. The process of making revisions to a HTML document is simplified and the cost of serving a wide range of platforms is reduced.

2. Consider universal accessibility

The Web page author is recommended to consider that their HTML documents may be accessed from a variety of special platforms by those users with physical limitations.

Many HTML 4 tags have attributes, such as "label", that can be set to provide extra information for these users.

Also, with increasing globalization, a HTML document may be reaching a far-off audience that has different computer configurations to those of the originating computer.

Consequently, for documents to be interpreted correctly, the Web page author should include in their document information about the natural language used, direction of the text and how the document is encoded.

3. Speed-up table rendering

The table layout model in previous versions of HTML often had to download the complete table data before the browser was able to render the table in the display.

Web page authors are recommended to make use of the new table model in HTML 4 which has added features to help browsers render tables more quickly.

The Document Head

This chapter explores the head section of a HTML 4 page and illustrates by example how it can be used. The samples show how to describe features of the HTML document and how to add scripts and style sheets to the page.

Covers

Chapter Two

Inside the Head

The head section of a HTML document follows the obligatory Document Type Definition (DTD) and is used to contain information about that document.

Typically this will include the document title and keywords that can be used by search engines to describe the document.

The document head may also contain script code and style sheets to determine how the contents should be presented.

For more about tag attributes see page 44.

In HTML 4 the entire head section may be contained within a pair of <head> </head> tags although these are entirely optional and only serve to group the head contents together.

When reading HTML code it does help to see the head section contents grouped by the <head> </head> tags so they are included in the examples given in this book.

The <head> tag may optionally contain a new attribute named "profile" to specify the location of a meta data profile to be used by the document.

The profile attribute is not widely used but is given here for completeness and may appear in the HTML code like this:

More details on meta data are given later in this chapter.

```
<!DOCTYPE HTML PUBLIC "-//W3C//DTD HTML 4.01//EN"
          "http://www.w3.org/TR/html4/strict.dtd">

<head
profile="http://www.purl.org/metadata/dublin_core">

        [ head section content goes here ]
</head>
```

Like many of the new features in HTML 4 the profile attribute has been included to accommodate possible future developments in the use of the language.

There are anticipated advances in the way that the HTML page may be viewed on a variety of browsers (user agents) such as cellphones, PDAs and other devices in addition to the traditional PC Web browser.

Document Title

Each HTML 4 document must specify a document title.

There may be only one title and this should be contained within a pair of <title> </title> tags in the head section of the document.

See page 62 for more on character entities.

The title may comprise of both regular text characters and character entities for special characters such as ampersand, copyright mark and accented characters.

Although the document title is not part of the actual document content the HTML 4 specification states that the user-agent (browser) must always make the document title available to the user.

For this reason it is recommended that the given title should be as descriptive as possible to help describe the document.

For example, a document entitled "Intro" merely suggests that the document is an introduction to something.

Whereas a title of "An Introduction to HTML 4" describes the content and the topic of that document.

Traditional PC Web browsers will display the document title in the title bar of the browser window as seen below:

```
<!DOCTYPE HTML PUBLIC "-//W3C//DTD HTML 4.01//EN"
         "http://www.w3.org/TR/html4/strict.dtd">
<head>
<title>An Introduction to HTML 4</title>
</head>
```

Meta Information

Meta information is simply data that describes other data.

In the context of a HTML document meta data describes the document itself rather than the document content.

Meta data is defined in the head section of a document using the HTML 4 <meta> tag.

The <meta> tag is only used to declare data in its attributes so it does not have an associated closing tag.

 The other possible attribute in the <meta> tag is "scheme" - see an example on page 25.

Most <meta> tags use the "content" and "http-equiv" attributes or the "content" and "name" attributes.

The http-equiv attribute can specify a data type to the server while the content attribute specifies the data itself.

For example, the "Expires" data type can be used to force a Web browser to download the latest version of a Web page.

Ordinarily a Web browser will load a cached copy of a Web page location if one is available in the browser's cache.

Using a meta tag the page can be set to expire so that the browser will seek the latest version from the server if the current date exceeds that specified by the content attribute.

The following example sets a page to expire at midnight on New Year's Eve 2003. It is important to specify the date in the exact format that is used in this example:

```
<!DOCTYPE HTML PUBLIC "-//W3C//DTD HTML 4.01//EN"
        "http://www.w3.org/TR/html4/strict.dtd">
<head>
<title>This Page Expires After 2003</title>
<meta http-equiv="Expires"
    content="Wed, 31 Dec 2003 23:59:59 GMT">
</head>
```

It should be noted that the use of a <meta> tag "Refresh" to redirect users to another location is not recommended. Redirects should instead use a server script because some browsers do not support the <meta> "Refresh" method.

Character Encoding

A <meta> tag can advise the browser of the character encoding used by the document content.

The http-equiv attribute is assigned as "Content-type" so the content attribute can then describe the document content.

The content should firstly be described as "text/html;" to tell the browser to expect to receive HTML content. Then the character encoding is specified as "charset=[character set]".

There are literally dozens of character sets in use but the table below lists some of the most commonly found ones and the example specifies the Shift_JIS character encoding.

Name	Character Set
US-ASCII	US ASCII characters
ISO 8859-1	Standard ISO Latin-1 characters
UTF-8	Multi-lingual Universal Transformation Format
Shift_JIS	Japanese characters
Big5	Chinese traditional characters

Remember the semi-colon after the code "text/html".

```
<!DOCTYPE HTML PUBLIC "-//W3C//DTD HTML 4.01//EN"
          "http://www.w3.org/TR/html4/strict.dtd">
<head>
<title>Using SHIFT_JIS Encoding</title>
<meta http-equiv="Content-type"
      content="text/html; charset=Shift_JIS">
</head>
```

Search-Engine Meta Data

Search engines are used by the main Internet portal sites, such as Yahoo, to return resulting links to documents containing keywords that have been entered by the user.

The methods used by the search engines vary and are constantly being updated to ensure variety of results.

Most search engines do however use, in part at least, the <meta> data provided in a document head section to return a link to that document for the user.

The two pieces of meta data sought by search engines are the document "keywords" and "description".

To make a document visible to search engines it is important to include both of these correctly.

Use only lowercase characters for keywords as most users use these and some search engines are case-sensitive.

The keywords should appear in a <meta> tag that uses a name attribute to specify the term "keywords". The content attribute of this tag should be assigned a short list of relevant topical words that do actually appear in the page content, and listed preferably in the order in which they appear.

The description should appear in a <meta> tag that uses a name attribute to specify the term "description". The content attribute of this tag should be assigned an accurate description of the document in less than 25 words.

In the following example the document head contains meta data to assist the search engine user who is seeking information for a Greek holiday:

```
<!DOCTYPE HTML PUBLIC "-//W3C//DTD HTML 4.01//EN"
        "http://www.w3.org/TR/html4/strict.dtd">
<head>
<title>Greek Island Sunshine Holidays</title>
<meta name="keywords"
      content="Greek,Greece,holiday,sunshine">
<meta name="description"
      content="Idyllic Sunny Greek Holidays">
</head>
```

Custom Meta Data

More advanced use of meta data allows the document author to specify any custom properties of the document that may be useful to a browser.

For example, in a document describing this book it may be useful to add some of the relevant information as meta data:

The examples given here will illustrate some advanced uses of meta data.

```
<!DOCTYPE HTML PUBLIC "-//W3C//DTD HTML 4.01//EN"
        "http://www.w3.org/TR/html4/strict.dtd">
<head>
<title>HTML 4 in easy steps</title>
<meta name="author" content="Mike McGrath">
<meta name="ISBN" content="1-84078-048-7">
</head>
```

This ability to add any custom values to the <meta> tag attributes will only be useful if they can be recognized.

One major effort to consolidate meta data involves a profile standard called the "Dublin Core" that defines a set of recommended properties to describe books.

Current information about this profile together with full specifications can be found on the Web at http://purl.org/dc.

The properties that are defined by a profile have their values set by subsequent <meta> tags within the document.

The <meta> tag also has a "scheme" attribute that can be used in conjunction with a profile to help the browser correctly interpret the meta data.

In the example below a hypothetical profile defines a scheme to specify the format of an ISBN book number:

```
<!DOCTYPE HTML PUBLIC "-//W3C//DTD HTML 4.01//EN"
        "http://www.w3.org/TR/html4/strict.dtd">
<head profile="http://acme.com/bookprofile">
<title>HTML 4 in easy steps</title>
<meta scheme="ISBN" name="identifier"
      content="1-84078-048-7">
</head>
```

Adding Scripts

Scripts can be added to a HTML 4 document to interact with the user and provide dynamic content.

The script must be contained by <script> </script> tags and it is convenient to locate scripts in the document head.

A <script> attribute called "type" should specify the scripting language to be used such as "text/javascript".

In order to avoid the script appearing as displayed text in those browsers that do not recognise the <script> tag the script block should start with "<!--" and end with "//-->".

Alternative content can be set outside the head with <noscript> tags for browsers that do not recognise scripts:

The text output by the script is contained by a set of HTML 4 <p> </p> tags to denote a paragraph – see page 31 for more details.

```
<!DOCTYPE HTML PUBLIC "-//W3C//DTD HTML 4.01//EN"
            "http://www.w3.org/TR/html4/strict.dtd">
<head>
<title>A Simple JavaScript Example</title>
<script type="text/javascript">
<!--
document.write("<p>Hello from JavaScript</p>");
//-->
</script>
</head>
<noscript><p>Document uses JavaScript</p></noscript>
```

Scripts in remote files can be included with the <script> tag by adding a "src" attribute giving the location of the file:

```
<script type="text/javascript" src="myscript.js">
</script>
```

Adding Style Sheets

Style sheets can be added to a HTML 4 document head to influence how the document content should be displayed.

The style sheet rules that define how the content should appear must be enclosed by <style> </style> tags.

Also the style sheet language must be specified by the "type" attribute of the <style> tag such as "text/css".

In order to avoid the rules appearing as displayed text in those browsers that do not recognise the <style> tag the style sheet should start with "<!--" and end with "//-->".

The following example builds upon the example on the previous page to add style to the text output from the script.

This style sheet sets the overall height of the text and forces the first letter to be double the height of the other text:

 This example is just to illustrate how to add a style sheet to a document. Full examples of style sheet rules are given later in this book.

```
<!DOCTYPE HTML PUBLIC "-//W3C//DTD HTML 4.01//EN"
            "http://www.w3.org/TR/html4/strict.dtd">
<head>
<title>A JavaScript Example With Style</title>
<style type="text/css">
<!--
p { font-size: 12pt }
p:first-letter { font-size: 200% }
//-->
</style>
<script type="text/javascript">
<!--
document.write("<p>Hello from JavaScript</p>");
//-->
</script>  </head>
```

Linking Resources

The HTML 4 <link> tag provides a means to link resources, such as an external style sheet, to the document.

This tag can only be used in the head section of a document but each head section can contain many <link> tags. Each of these are used to specify three attributes that define a resource type, location and relationship.

A "href" attribute specifies the location, a "rel" attribute specifies the relationship to the document and a "type" attribute states the type of resource as one of the following:

Stylesheet	Alternate	Start	Next	Prev
Contents	Index	Glossary	Copyright	Chapter
Section	Subsection	Appendix	Help	Bookmark

The example below has a <link> tag to add an external style sheet and another <link> tag to provide information of where a search engine can find the next page:

Both <base> and <link> tags do not have any closing tags.

```
<!DOCTYPE HTML PUBLIC "-//W3C//DTD HTML 4.01//EN"
          "http://www.w3.org/TR/html4/strict.dtd">
<head>
<title>The History Of The World - Page 1</title>
<base href="http://domain.com/docs/page1.html">
<link href="a.css" rel="stylesheet" type="text/css">
<link href="page2.html" rel="next" type="text/html">
</head>
```

Notice that the example uses a HTML 4 <base> tag to define the path to be used by subsequent pages.

For this reason the <base> tag, if present, must be situated in the head section before mention of any other addresses.

The base path is by default that of the current document but using a <base> tag enables files located in the specified base directory to be addressed by just their file names.

Body Text Content

This chapter demonstrates how to incorporate text content into the body section of a HTML document. All of the layout tags available in HTML 4 are described and examples of each one illustrate how they control the displayed text.

Covers

Chapter Three

The Document Body

Following the obligatory DTD and the head section code the HTML 4 document arrives at the document body where the actual content is written.

The HTML 4 specification does still have <body> </body> tags but these are now optional. Also the <body> attributes formerly used in HTML to specify background colour, text colour and hyperlink colours have all been made obsolete.

See chapter 4 for details on how to specify body colours in style sheets.

All of these colours should now be specified in a style sheet.

The only two <body> attributes that remain fully valid in HTML 4 are "onload" and "onunload" that can be used to run script functions when the document loads and unloads.

This example illustrates the document body section and calls an alert function when the page loads and unloads:

```
<!DOCTYPE HTML PUBLIC "-//W3C//DTD HTML 4.01//EN"
          "http://www.w3.org/TR/html4/strict.dtd">
<head>
<title>Using Load And Onunload</title>
</head>

<body onload="alert('Hi!')" onunload="alert('Bye')">

         [ document content goes here ]
</body>
```

Further code examples may exclude the DTD and head to save space.

Content in Paragraphs

Text content is traditionally separated into sentences and paragraphs to be more easily read and understood.

The basic HTML 4 tags that define the document text content into paragraphs are the <p> </p> tags.

These will visually separate the displayed text, normally leaving two empty lines between each paragraph.

Some browsers may ignore paragraphs that do not have a </p> closing tag.

Although browsers may correctly render text into paragraphs without the closing </p> tag its omission is bad practice.

The closing </p> tag should always be included as shown in the example below and throughout this book:

```
<body>

<p>In the midst of all its busy city life, Heraklion
has a number of interesting and endearing features.
</p>

<p>
One is the Venetian harbour - a good place to begin
a tour of the city.
</p>

</body>
```

Forcing Line Breaks

When the body content is displayed text will, by default, wrap automatically to the next line after meeting the right-hand edge of the display area.

The browser will normally seek back in the text to find the last space at which to break the line.

This ensures that the line wraps intelligently so that the last whole word on the line is not broken.

A line break in the displayed text can be forced using the HTML 4 <br> single tag.

The <br> tag is always used without a closing tag.

This tag can be inserted as often as required and at any point in the text to force one or more line breaks.

In the following example the <br> tag is used to determine how the body text content should appear:

*Use the code

 to add a double line space between displayed text.*

```
<body>
<p>
The top attraction in Heraklion is
<br>
the Venetian Castle,
<br>
still known by its Turkish name "Koúles".
</p>
</body>
```

Forcing Line Breaks

File   Edit   View   Favorites   Tools   Help

The top attraction in Heraklion is
the Venetian Castle,
still known by its Turkish name "Koúles".

Quotes and Blockquotes

In the HTML 4 specifications two tags are provided for the display of quotations within document body text content.

The <q> </q> quote tags allow for short snippets of quoted text to be inserted into regular text content.

See page 62 for how to use quotation marks inside normal text.

Whereas the <blockquote> </blockquote> tags can be used to insert longer quotations into the body text.

Both of these tags accept a single attribute called "cite" that can be assigned an address indicating the quotes source.

Most browsers will render the <blockquote> content as an indented text as seen in the example below.

This indentation should not be used for presentational purposes though as not all browsers will act the same.

It is the intent of the HTML 4 specification that the browser should provide quotation marks to surround content in each of these tags, although most may not fully comply.

```
<body>
<p>Alexander spoke solemnly...</p>
<blockquote cite="http://domain.com/plutarch.html"
<p>If I were not Alexander, I would be Diogenes.</p>
</blockquote>
<p>according to Plutarch.</p>
</body>
```

Headings

Headings in HTML 4 documents are used to define sections of text in the same way as the heading on this page.

There are six sets of heading tags available in HTML 4 that range from <h1> </h1> as the most important, down to <h6> </h6> as the least important.

Browsers will generally display headings in increasingly larger fonts to emphasise their importance.

In addition the browser could use the document headings to compile a list of topics that appear in that document.

The simple example below illustrates each of the headings as they appear when viewed in Microsoft Internet Explorer:

Heading tags automatically add a line break to move onto the next line.

```
<body>

<h1>H1 Heading</h1>
<h2>H2 Heading</h2>
<h3>H3 Heading</h3>
<h4>H4 Heading</h4>
<h5>H5 Heading</h5>
<h6>H6 Heading</h6>

</body>
```

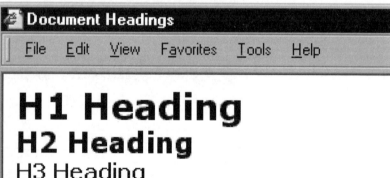

Emphasising Text

The text displayed in the body of a HTML 4 document can be emphasized by making the font appear bolder, or in italic style, or in both bold and italic style.

To make the text bold requires the text to be contained inside a pair of <b> </b> tags. Alternatively emphasis can be suggested using HTML 4 <strong> </strong> tags that will generally display the text in a bold font.

For italic text the <i> </i> tags must surround the text. Or emphasis can be suggested using HTML 4 <em> </em> tags that will generally display the text in an italic font.

Bold and italic text can be displayed by nesting one pair of tags inside the other as illustrated by this example:

Take care to close nested tags in the correct order to avoid errors –
<b><i>text</b></i> is wrong.

```
<body>
<p>This regular text can become<br> <b>bold</b> or
<i>italic</i> or <b> <i>bold italic</i> </b>
</p>
<p>This regular text can become<br>
<strong>strong</strong> or <em>em(phasized)</em> <br>
or <strong> <em>strongly emphasized</em> </strong>
</p>
</body>
```

Text Formatting

Text in the body of a HTML 4 document will generally, by default, be displayed in the variable width font and font size selected by the user in the browser settings.

The <tt> </tt> tags can be used to force the browser to display text using the fixed width font selected by the user.

Font size can be varied using the <big> </big> tags to display text in a font size that is larger than the font that is used by default for regular text.

Also the <small> </small> tags may be used to display text in a font size that is smaller than that used for regular text.

The example below illustrates how text appearance can be formatted into fixed width font and a variety of font sizes:

Use multiple <big> or <small> tags for greater change away from the default font size.

```
<body>

<p>You can to see the high points of Heraklion
<br>
<tt>-the Archaeological Museum and Knossos-</tt>
<br>in a very <big>full</big> day.
<br>
<small><small>
But then you'd be missing the best of Crete.
</small></small>
</p>

</body>
```

Preformatted Text

The HTML 4 <pre> tag is useful to retain the format characteristics of preformatted text within a document.

Any text within <pre> </pre> tags will be displayed to include the original spaces, tabs and line breaks that are collectively known as "whitespace".

The browser will not generally wrap preformatted text and may display the text in a fixed width font, as illustrated in the example shown below:

The variable and fixed-width fonts are determined by the user's browser option settings.

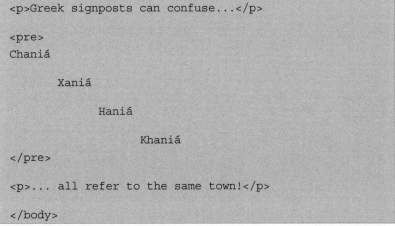

```
<body>

<p>Greek signposts can confuse...</p>

<pre>
Chaniá

        Xaniá

                Haniá

                        Khaniá
</pre>

<p>... all refer to the same town!</p>

</body>
```

Subscript and Superscript

The HTML 4 <sub> and <sup> tags can be used to display text that is vertically altered from the regular text line.

For subscript text the tags display text shifted down by about half the line height of regular text.

Similarly the tags display superscript text shifted up by about half the line height of the regular text.

It should be noted that, although the position is shifted, the text is displayed normally in the same font throughout.

The subscript and superscript tags are especially useful for the display of some foreign language texts.

The example below illustrates both subscript and superscript displaying text with altered vertical alignment:

The <small> tag could be used to reduce the font for the "2" in the first line.

```
<body>

<p>
The chemical symbol H<sub>2</sub>O represents water.
<br>
In the West 1<sup>st</sup> January is New Years Day.
<br>
Surfers ride the w<sup>a</sup>v<sub>e</sub>s
on the ocean.
</p>

</body>
```

Subscript And Superscript

File   Edit   View   Favorites   Tools   Help

The chemical symbol H_2O represents water.
In the West 1st January is New Years Day.
Surfers ride the w^av_es on the ocean.

Contact Address

The HTML 4 <address> tag can be used to supply contact information regarding a document.

It may often be found at the start or end of a document providing a link to a page giving more information about the author of that document.

For more on hyperlinks see chapter 7.

It could also be used to provide information regarding the authorship of a particular form within a document.

In the example below the <address> tag incorporates a hyperlink to another page about the document's author:

```
<body>

<h3>Fun With HTML 4</h3>

<p>The latest specification of HTML is great.</p>

<address>
This article by:
<a href="mikem.html">Mike McGrath</a> <br>
Your comments are welcome.
</address>

</body>
```

With this example the browser has automatically chosen to display any text within the <address> tag in italic font.

Displaying Code in Text

HTML 4 specifications provide three tags for the specific purpose of describing pieces of computer programming code when it is to be displayed in a document.

The <code> </code> tags are used to denote that the text contained between the tags is indeed programming code.

Reference in the general document text to instances of a variable in the programming code may use <var> </var> tags to denote a program variable.

Any samples of text output from a program can be denoted in the document text by the <samp> </samp> tags.

The example below uses these tags to describe a simple JavaScript program in the general document text:

The <var> tag only denotes that the text is describing a program variable – it does not declare a variable for use in HTML 4.

```
<body>

<p>When this simple JavaScript is run:</p>
<p><code>var content="Hello";<br>
document.write(content);</code></p>
<p>the <var>content</var>
is written as <samp>Hello</samp> on the page.
</p>

</body>
```

Advisory Tags

The tags <abbr> </abbr> and <acronym> </acronym> can be used to denote abbreviations and acronyms.

These tags may be useful, for example, to exclude the tag contents from a spell checker.

The <dfn> </dfn> tags can be used to indicate the definitive meaning for a given term and <cite> </cite> tags may be used as a reference to another source.

Also <kbd> </kbd> tags indicate text that a user can input.

All of these tags are illustrated in the example below that assigns a meaningful value to the title attribute of each tag:

Browsers choose how to use the given information – here Internet Explorer displays the title value as a "tooltip" when the cursor is over the text.

```
<body>

<p>You can learn
<abbr title="Common Gateway Interface">CGI</abbr>
scripting with
<acronym title="Practical Enquiry and Reporting
Language">Perl</acronym> from <br>
<dfn title="PerlBook">"CGI & Perl in Easy Steps"</dfn>
by <cite title="mikem.html">Mike McGrath</cite>
</p>

<p>Press <kbd title="agree">Y</kbd>
on your keyboard for more details.</p>

</body>
```

Delete and Insert

The HTML 4 specification has two special tags that can be used to identify text that has been deleted or inserted in respect of an earlier version of that document.

This may be particularly appropriate when updating draft documents to reveal the changes.

The <del> </del> and <ins> </ins> tags used for this purpose are unusual as they can be applied in two ways.

Firstly the tags can be applied "in-line" to a word or several words in a paragraph as usual.

Also they can be used to contain entire paragraphs, lists and tables that have been changed.

This example uses these tags in-line to change "1" into "2" and then to change a complete paragraph:

The tags define the changed text but the browser will decide how to utilise this information.

```
<body>

<p>
The option permits <del>1</del> <ins>2</ins> selections.
</p>

<del> <p>This is the first draft content.</p> </del>

<ins> <p>This is the second draft content.</p> </ins>

</body>
```

Adding Style to Content

This chapter introduces tag attributes and the principles of style sheets as a means to determine the presentation of content. Examples illustrate how HTML 4 tags can define pieces of text content so that the style sheet may specify how each piece of text should be displayed.

Covers

Chapter Four

About Tag Attributes

Attributes are features of the HTML 4 specification that can be added inside individual tags to make them more useful.

To add an attribute to a tag requires that the attribute name is added inside the tag followed by "=" and a given value.

Tags that can be used in the document body to display content can accept any of the attributes listed in this table:

Tags used for information about the document have other attributes - see examples in chapter 2.

Attribute	Specifies
id	document-wide unique id name for element
class	class name to apply associated style rules
style	simple in-line style rule
lang	language in short coded form
dir	direction of text either rtl or ltr
onclick	mouse click action
ondblclick	mouse double-click action
onmousedown	mouse button pressed action
onmouseup	mouse button released action
onmouseover	pointer moves on element action
onmouseout	pointer moves off element action
onmousemove	pointer moves within element action
onkeypress	key pressed and released action
onkeydown	key pressed action
onkeyup	key released action

These attributes cannot be used inside tags that are used to denote information about the document such as <base>, <head>, <meta>, <param>, <style> and <script>.

Using Tag Attributes

To use a tag attribute its name must be added inside the tag together with an assigned value enclosed within quotes.

In the table opposite all tag attributes that begin with "on" assign "event-handlers" that will perform an action each time a particular event occurs.

The event-handler will normally be a script function that will perform the desired action.

A piece of document text can have a style rule applied in-line with the HTML 4 <style> tag. It is better to use a style sheet though to keep all the style rules together.

Multiple attributes can be added inside a single tag.

This example adds a style attribute to apply a style rule to the font and adds an onclick attribute that will open an alert dialog whenever the onclick event occurs:

Always use a style sheet to apply rules rather than the style attribute.

```
<!DOCTYPE HTML PUBLIC "-//W3C//DTD HTML 4.01//EN"
            "http://www.w3.org/TR/html4/strict.dtd">

<head> <title>Using Tag Attributes</title> </head>
<body>
<p style="font-family:fantasy"
   onclick="alert('Mouse Clicked')">Click Here
</p>
</body>
```

A First Style Sheet

Style sheets are used in HTML 4 documents to influence how aspects of the document content should be displayed.

The code that determines how each part of the content should appear is referred to as the style sheet "rules".

Style sheet rules must be located in the style sheet block that is situated in the head section of a HTML document.

The syntax of a style sheet rule first states the part of the content to affect followed by a list of its attributes and values inside a pair of curly brackets ("{ }").

Attribute names must be recognised for the stated document part and the assigned value must be valid for that attribute.

Each attribute and its value are separated by a colon and each "attribute:value" pair is terminated with a semi-colon.

This example applies style sheet rules to the document body itself to create a black background with all text in white:

The trailing semi-colon can be omitted if the style rule specifies just one attribute:value pair.

```
<!DOCTYPE HTML PUBLIC "-//W3C//DTD HTML 4.01//EN"
           "http://www.w3.org/TR/html4/strict.dtd">
<head>
<title>Body Styling</title>
<style type="text/css">
<!--
body { background-color:black; color:white; }
//-->
</style>
</head>

<body> <p>This is a first style sheet.</p> </body>
```

Styling Tags

Style sheet rules can be applied to a selected tag so that each occurrence of that tag in the document content is affected.

This example changes the font for all <h3> tag content:

This example does not change the h2 heading or any other text font.

```
<!DOCTYPE HTML PUBLIC "-//W3C//DTD HTML 4.01//EN"
            "http://www.w3.org/TR/html4/strict.dtd">
<head> <title>Tag Styling</title>
<style type="text/css">
<!--
h3 { font-family:monospace; }
//-->
</style> </head>
<body>
<h2>Museums</h2> <h3>Archaeological Museum</h3>
<p>The most important collection of Minoan art and
artefacts in the world.</p>
<h3>Historical Museum</h3>
<p>The history of Crete from Byzantine to modern times.
</p>
</body>
```

Style sheets are more fully called Cascading Style Sheets after the way a style rule "cascades" through a document, applying presentational qualities to each instance of its specified element.

Styling with Class

All HTML 4 tags that are used to display content can accept an attribute called "class" to which a name can be assigned.

The class name can be used in a style sheet to apply rules so that any tag bearing that class name will apply its rules.

The example below defines a class named "myclass" with a rule to change content to a monospace font. The "myclass" style is applied to the top heading and the bottom paragraph:

The class name must be preceded by a full stop when it is being defined in the style sheet.

```
<!DOCTYPE HTML PUBLIC "-//W3C//DTD HTML 4.01//EN"
          "http://www.w3.org/TR/html4/strict.dtd">
<head> <title>Class Styling</title>
<style type="text/css">
<!--
.myclass { font-family:monospace; }
//-->
</style> </head> <body>
<h3 class="myclass">Archaeological Museum</h3>
<p>The most important collection of Minoan art and
artefacts in the world.</p>
<h3>Historical Museum</h3>
<p class="myclass">The history of Crete from Byzantine
to modern times.</p>
</body>
```

Styling with Identity

All HTML 4 tags that are used to display content can accept an attribute called "id" to which a name can be assigned.

The id name can be used to identify that individual tag in a style sheet defining rules for how its content should appear.

In the example below all three paragraphs are assigned id names but only two of those are used in the style sheet to assign rules to their contents:

The id name must be preceded by a hash mark (#) when defining rules in the style sheet block.

```
<!DOCTYPE HTML PUBLIC "-//W3C//DTD HTML 4.01//EN"
          "http://www.w3.org/TR/html4/strict.dtd">
<head>
<title>Id Styling</title>
<style type="text/css">
<!--
#para2 { font-family:cursive; }
#para3 { font-family:serif; }
//-->
</style>
</head>
<body>
<p id="para1">Paragraph 1 - Default</p>
<p id="para2">Paragraph 2 - Cursive</p>
<p id="para3">Paragraph 3 - Serif</p>
</body>
```

Colours

When assigning colours in HTML 4 the colour should be specified as a hexadecimal number preceded by a hash mark.

This six figure number represents the Red-Green-Blue (RGB) components that make up the whole colour.

The first two numbers are its red component value, the second two numbers are its green component value and the third two numbers are its blue component value.

A hexadecimal colour number that has zero RGB values creates Black with the hexadecimal number of #000000.

Conversely a hexadecimal number that has all maximum RGB values creates White with the hexadecimal #FFFFFF.

To create a red hexadecimal value you can use maximum R value plus zero GB values to produce hexadecimal #FF0000.

HTML 4 also recognises the following 16 colours by name:

Spellings must be US versions so "colour" must become "color" and "grey" must become "gray".

Name	Hexadecimal	Name	Hexadecimal
Black	#000000	Green	#008000
Silver	#C0C0C0	Lime	#00FF00
Gray	#808080	Olive	#808000
White	#FFFFFF	Yellow	#FFFF00
Maroon	#800000	Navy	#000080
Red	#FF0000	Blue	#0000FF
Purple	#800080	Teal	#008080
Fuchsia	#FF00FF	Aqua	#00FFFF

To assign any colour a style sheet must be used with the hexadecimal number or the colour name if one of the above.

So "color:red;" and "color:#FF0000;" are both valid rules.

Applying Colour Style

This example applies font and colour style rules to two paragraphs in the document body.

The first rule in the style sheet changes the font for all paragraphs in the document.

Next the background and text colours are specified for the top paragraph using recognized name values.

Lastly the background and text colours are specified for the bottom paragraph using hexadecimal number values:

Internet Explorer sets the paragraph boundary across the page – other browsers may define the boundaries of the paragraph differently.

```html
<!DOCTYPE HTML PUBLIC "-//W3C//DTD HTML 4.01//EN"
          "http://www.w3.org/TR/html4/strict.dtd">

<head>
<title>Applying Colour Style</title>
<style type="text/css">
<!--
p { font-family:cursive; }
#para1 { color:black; background-color:silver; }
#para2 { color:#FFFFFF; background-color:#000000; }
//-->
</style>
</head>
<body>
<p id="para1">Paragraph 1 - Black on Silver</p>
<p id="para2">Paragraph 2 - White on Black</p>
</body>
```

Dividing Content

The document body can be divided into blocks by grouping its content elements with the HTML 4 <div> </div> tags.

This is very useful to control page layout as the style characteristics of each block can be set by style sheet rules.

The <div> tag can have id and class attributes that may be used in the style sheet to specify style requirements.

This example sets the background colour of all <div> elements and the absolute position of two <div> blocks:

An absolutely positioned block will always maintain its set position regardless of other content.

```
<!DOCTYPE HTML PUBLIC "-//W3C//DTD HTML 4.01//EN"
            "http://www.w3.org/TR/html4/strict.dtd">
<head> <title>Controlling Block Layout</title>
<style type="text/css">
<!--
div { background-color:silver; }
#div1 { position:absolute; top:0px; left:0px; }
#div2 { position:absolute; top:30px; left:120px; }
//-->
</style>
</head>
<body>
<div id="div1"> <p>Paragraph 1</p> </div>
<div id="div2">
<p>Paragraph 2</p> <p>Paragraph 3</p>
</div>
</body>
```

Centring with Style

In HTML 4 the previous <center> tag, that was used to centre content, has been made obsolete.

The style sheet is now used to centre document content.

An entire document can be made to align its content centrally by applying a style sheet rule to its document body.

Individual blocks of content can be made to align their content by applying a style sheet rule to the <div> element.

In this example three blocks are centred on the page with each controlling alignment of their text individually:

Notice that there are automatic line breaks after each <div> block, but no line spaces between them.

```
<!DOCTYPE HTML PUBLIC "-//W3C//DTD HTML 4.01//EN"
            "http://www.w3.org/TR/html4/strict.dtd">
<head> <title>Style Alignment</title>
<style type="text/css">
<!--
body { text-align:center; }
div { width:150; background-color:silver; }
#div1 { text-align:left; }
#div2 { text-align:center; }
#div3 { text-align:right;}
//-->
</style> </head>
<body>
<div id="div1"><p>Paragraph 1</p></div>
<div id="div2"><p>Paragraph 2</p></div>
<div id="div3"><p>Paragraph 3</p></div>
</body>
```

Inline Styling

Style rules can be applied to small pieces of text "in-line" with the HTML 4 <span> </span> tags.

These tags allow both id and class attributes to apply style sheet rules without automatically adding line breaks.

Unlike the <div> blocks that can be used to control block layout the <span> tag is not used for positioning but rather to set display characteristics for short pieces of text.

This example uses <span> tags to set the appearance of two pieces of text within a paragraph that is contained in a block:

The <span> tag can also accept attributes for intrinsic events such as onmouseover and onclick, that can be used with scripts for dynamic effects.

```
<!DOCTYPE HTML PUBLIC "-//W3C//DTD HTML 4.01//EN"
          "http://www.w3.org/TR/html4/strict.dtd">
<head> <title>Span Styling</title>
<style type="text/css">
<!--
#div1{width:220; background-color:silver; padding:5px;}
#span1{ background-color:black;color:white;
        font-weight:bold; }
#span2{ background-color:white; color:black;
        font-style:italic; }
//-->
</style> </head> <body>
<div id="div1"> <p>The road descends to
<span id="span1">Agios Nikolaos</span>
offering magnificent views of the
<span id="span2">Bay of Mirabello</span> </p> </div>
</body>
```

Lists and Entities

This chapter illustrates by example how HTML 4 can be used to display different types of lists in a variety of ways. There are also examples to demonstrate how entities can be used to add non-alphanumeric characters to the text.

Covers

Chapter Five

Unordered Lists

A list of items that does not require the items to be numbered in order is known as an "unordered" list.

In HTML 4 the <ul> </ul> tags are used to contain the items in an unordered list.

Each list item should be surrounded by <li> </li> tags, but the closing tag may optionally be omitted.

Browsers will choose how the list is to be presented but generally they will indent the list from other text.

Unordered lists will start each item with a default bullet point selected by the browser.

The following example illustrates an unordered list that is indented with bullet points marking each list item:

Use the </li> closing tag to make the code more readable.

```
<!DOCTYPE HTML PUBLIC "-//W3C//DTD HTML 4.01//EN"
            "http://www.w3.org/TR/html4/strict.dtd">
<head> <title>Unordered List</title> </head>
<body>
<p>First Unordered List:</p>
<ul>
<li>One</li>
<li>Two</li>
<li>Three</li>
</ul>
</body>
```

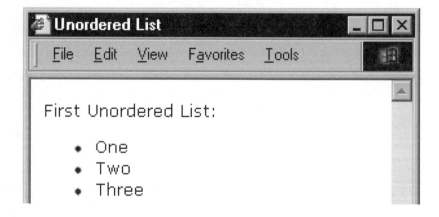

Bullet Point Styles

The style of bullet points to be used for marking items in an unordered list can be specified in the style sheet.

Bullet points may be either "circle", "square" or a filled circle called "disc".

This example illustrates each type of bullet point style:

Notice that the style sheet uses the id name of each list to apply the rule.

```
<!DOCTYPE HTML PUBLIC "-//W3C//DTD HTML 4.01//EN"
            "http://www.w3.org/TR/html4/strict.dtd">
<head>
<title>Bullet Point Styles</title>
<style type="text/css">
<!--
#list1 { list-style-type:disc; }
#list2 { list-style-type:circle; }
#list3 { list-style-type:square; }
//-->
</style>
</head>
<body>
<ul id="list1"><li>Disc 1</li><li>Disc 2</li></ul>
<ul id="list2"><li>Circle 1</li><li>Circle 2</li></ul>
<ul id="list3"><li>Square 1</li><li>Square 2</li></ul>
</body>
```

Ordered Lists

A list of items that has each item numbered to note its position in the list is called an "ordered" list.

In HTML 4 the <ol> </ol> tags are used to contain the items in an ordered list.

Each list item should be enclosed within <li> </li> tags and will be numbered in the default manner of the browser.

All lists can be nested, as seen in this example that demonstrates two nested ordered lists:

The </li> tag may be omitted but its inclusion makes the code more readable.

```
<!DOCTYPE HTML PUBLIC "-//W3C//DTD HTML 4.01//EN"
          "http://www.w3.org/TR/html4/strict.dtd">
<head> <title>Ordered Lists</title> </head>
<body>
<p>First Ordered Lists:</p>
<ol>
<li>One</li>
<li>Two</li>
<li><ol>
    <li>Alpha</li>
    <li>Bravo</li>
    <li>Charlie</li>
    </ol></li>
<li>Three</li>
</ol>
</body>
```

Numbering Styles

The style of numbering in an ordered list can be specified as Arabic numbers, lowercase Roman numbers, uppercase Roman numbers, lowercase alpha characters or uppercase alpha characters. Each style is shown in this example:

Class attributes apply the style sheet rules to the entire first list and to each item in the nested list.

```
<!DOCTYPE HTML PUBLIC "-//W3C//DTD HTML 4.01//EN"
            "http://www.w3.org/TR/html4/strict.dtd">
<head> <title>Numbering Styles</title>
<style type="text/css">
<!--
.arab { list-style-type:arabic-numbers; }
.lwrR { list-style-type:lower-roman; }
.uprR { list-style-type:upper-roman; }
.lwrA { list-style-type:lower-alpha; }
.uprA { list-style-type:upper-alpha; }
//-->
</style> </head>

<body> <ol class="lwrR">
<li>Lower Roman</li> <li>Lower Roman</li>
    <li><ol><li class="uprR">Upper Roman</li>
        <li class="arab">Arabic</li>
        <li class="lwrA">Lower Alpha</li>
        <li class="uprA">Upper Alpha</li> </ol></li>
<li>Lower Roman</li>
</ol> </body>
```

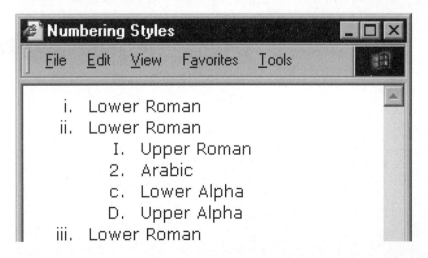

Definition Lists

A HTML 4 definition list is a unique type of list where each list item consists of a term and a definition.

All the list items are contained within <dl> </dl> tags.

The HTML 4 <dt> </dt> tags are used to contain a list term while <dd> </dd> tags contain a list definition.

Use closing tags </dt> and </dd> to make the code more easily readable.

Closing tags are optional for both <dt> and <dd> tags.

The browser will choose how to display a definition list but generally Web browsers will add a line break after the <dt> term and offset the <dd> definition.

In this example a definition list is used to display simple definitions of some popular Web languages:

```
<!DOCTYPE HTML PUBLIC "-//W3C//DTD HTML 4.01//EN"
          "http://www.w3.org/TR/html4/strict.dtd">
<head> <title>Definition List</title> </head> <body>
<dl>
<dt>HTML4:</dt>
<dd>Content markup language.</dd>
<dt>JavaScript:</dt>
<dd>Client-side scripting language.</dd>
<dt>Perl:<dt>
<dd>Server-side scripting language.</dd>
</dl> </body>
```

Use definition lists to display film scripts – where the <dt> term is the speaker's name, and the <dd> definition is the dialogue for that speaker.

Horizontal Rule

A horizontal ruled line can be drawn across the display area with the HTML 4 <hr> tag.

This tag is used alone without any closing tag.

The line will be drawn across the available display space excluding any margins or padding borders that it meets.

In the example below the first <hr> line fills the window width excluding margins while the second<hr> line fills the <div> block excluding padding borders:

The browser may choose how to display the <hr> line.

```
<!DOCTYPE HTML PUBLIC "-//W3C//DTD HTML 4.01//EN"
                "http://www.w3.org/TR/html4/strict.dtd">
<head>
<title>Horizontal Rule</title>
<style type="text/css">
<!--
#div1   {position:absolute; top:70; left:130; width:100;
border-style:double; border-width:3px; padding:5px; }
//-->
</style> </head>
<body>
<p>Section 1</p> <hr> <p>Section 2</p>
<div id="div1">Section 3<hr>Section 4</div>
</body>
```

Character Entities

The HTML 4 specification provides entities as a means to display characters that are meaningful in HTML itself.

This is necessary otherwise a "<" within the general text would be seen as the start of a HTML tag by the browser.

Entity references always start with a "&" ampersand and must be terminated by a semi-colon.

There are many character entities available in HTML 4 including the Greek alphabet in both upper and lower case.

Those most frequently used are shown in this example:

For a full list of all character entities see the HTML 4 Entity References at http://www.w3c.org.

```
<!DOCTYPE HTML PUBLIC "-//W3C//DTD HTML 4.01//EN"
              "http://www.w3.org/TR/html4/strict.dtd">
<head>
<title>Non Alpha-numeric Characters</title>
</head>

<body> <p>
Space Here<br>Ampersand &amp;<br>
Less Than &lt;<br>Greater Than &gt;<br>
Quote &quot;<br>Copyright &copy;<br>
Registered &reg;<br>Trademark &trade;
</p> </body>
```

Making Tables

This chapter describes the new table model introduced in HTML 4 that enables much faster display of table content. All the table tags are demonstrated to build a variety of tables that illustrate how to define rows, columns and cells.

Covers

Chapter Six

A Simple Table

Tables are used frequently to display information in HTML documents and are enclosed within <table> </table> tags.

Each piece of table data is contained in cells defined by the HTML 4 <td> </td> tags and each row of cells is contained in <tr> </tr> tags.

The <table> tag accepts an attribute named "border" to assign a width of border to surround the table and each cell.

A caption can be displayed with the table using <caption> </caption> tags. If this tag is used it must immediately follow the opening <table> tag.

The example below creates a table together with a caption.

This table displays a border one pixel wide and has one row containing three table data cells:

Later examples will build on this simple table as more table features are explained.

```
<body>

<table border="1">
<caption>A Simple Table</caption>
<tr>
   <td>Cell 1</td>
   <td>Cell 2</td>
   <td>Cell 3</td>
</tr>
</table>

</body>
```

Formatting Cells

Data in the table cells in the example opposite is positioned right up to the borders of each cell and the cells are spaced a short distance apart by default.

The appearance of the cell data can be improved by adding padding to each cell with a <table> "cellpadding" attribute. Also the spacing between cells may be specified with the <table> "cellspacing" attribute.

The background colour can be specified in HTML 4 tables with a "style" attribute. This attribute can be used in the <table>, <tr> and <td> tags to set the background colour respectively for the overall background, for a row of cells and the background colour of individual cells.

This example builds on the previous table to add cell padding and spacing plus background colour in two cells:

Assign a table border width of zero to hide all the table and cell borders.

```
<body>

<table border="1" cellpadding="5" cellspacing="5">
<caption>Formatting Cells</caption>
<tr>
   <td style="background-color:silver">Cell 1</td>
   <td>Cell 2</td>
   <td style="background-color:silver">Cell 3</td>
</tr>
</table>

</body>
```

Positioning the Table

To position a table on the page it should be contained within a <div> block to which an alignment style can be applied.

This allows a table to be positioned on the page just like any other block of document content.

The example below builds on the previous example to add a specific table width, using the <table> width attribute, and a <div> block to centre the table on the page:

The background colour of the cells is set for the entire row in the <tr> tag.

```
<!DOCTYPE HTML PUBLIC "-//W3C//DTD HTML 4.01//EN"
            "http://www.w3.org/TR/html4/strict.dtd">
<head> <title>Table #3</title>
<style type="text/css">
<!--
div { text-align:center; }
//-->
</style>
</head>

<body> <div>
<table border="1" width="250" cellpadding="5"
cellspacing="5">
<caption>Centred Table</caption>
<tr style="background-color:silver">
   <td>Cell 1</td><td>Cell 2</td><td>Cell 3</td>
</tr>
</table>
</div> </body>
```

Notice that although the table is central the text data in each cell is not.

Adding Rows

To add an additional row to a table requires another set of `<tr> </tr>` tags to be added containing the same number of `<td> </td>` cells as used in the first row.

This example builds on the previous example to add another row containing three cells and also adds another rule to the style sheet to centre the data in all cells:

The background colour is set for the entire table inside the `<table>` tag.

```
<!DOCTYPE HTML PUBLIC "-//W3C//DTD HTML 4.01//EN"
          "http://www.w3.org/TR/html4/strict.dtd">
<head> <title>Table #4</title>
<style type="text/css">
<!--
div { text-align:center; }
td { text-align:center; }
//-->
</style>
</head>
<body> <div>
<table border="1" style="background-color:silver"
width="220" cellpadding="5" cellspacing="5" >
<caption>Adding Rows</caption>
<tr><td>Cell 1</td><td>Cell 2</td><td>Cell 3</td></tr>
<tr><td>Cell 4</td><td>Cell 5</td><td>Cell 6</td></tr>
</table>
</div> </body>
```

Spanning Rows

A table cell can be made to span across a number of table rows with the <td> "rowspan" attribute. This attribute is assigned the number of rows to be spanned by the cell.

The cells being spanned in other rows must be removed.

In this example Cell 1 spans across two rows and Cell 4 has been removed:

This example builds on the previous example to show rowspan.

```
<!DOCTYPE HTML PUBLIC "-//W3C//DTD HTML 4.01//EN"
            "http://www.w3.org/TR/html4/strict.dtd">
<head> <title>Table #5</title>
<style type="text/css">
<!--
div { text-align:center; }
//-->
</style> </head>
<body> <div> <table border="1" style="background-color:
silver" width="220" cellpadding="5" cellspacing="5">
<caption>Cell Spanning Rows</caption>
<tr>
  <td rowspan="2">Cell 1</td>
  <td>Cell 2</td> <td>Cell 3</td>
</tr>
<tr> <td>Cell 5</td><td>Cell 6</td> </tr>
</table> </div> </body>
```

Spanning Columns

A table cell can be made to span across a number of table columns with the <td> "colspan" attribute. This attribute is assigned the number of columns to be spanned by the cell.

The cells being spanned in other columns must be removed.

In this example Cell 2 spans across two columns and Cell 3 has been removed:

This example builds on the previous example to show colspan.

```
<!DOCTYPE HTML PUBLIC "-//W3C//DTD HTML 4.01//EN"
            "http://www.w3.org/TR/html4/strict.dtd">
<head> <title>Table #6</title>
<style type="text/css">
<!--
div { text-align:center; }
//-->
</style> </head>
<body> <div> <table border="1" style="background-color:
silver" width="220" cellpadding="5" cellspacing="5">
<caption>Cell Spanning Columns</caption>
<tr>
   <td rowspan="2">Cell 1</td>
   <td colspan="2">Cell 2</td>
</tr>
<tr> <td>Cell 5</td><td>Cell 6</td> </tr>
</table> </div> </body>
```

Header and Footer

Extra rows can be added to the top and bottom of a table to display header and footer information.

The header row must be contained in <thead> </thead> tags and the footer row in tags named <tfoot> </tfoot>.

Cells in the header row may also use <th> </th> tags to contain their cell data instead of the usual <td> </td> tags. This will denote their data as header information.

When adding header and footer rows the rest of the regular rows must be contained within <tbody> </tbody> tags.

The simple table shown below includes a footer row and a header row containing column numbers:

The browser may choose to display header information in a different way to regular cell data.

```
<body>

<table border="1" cellpadding="2" cellspacing="1">
<thead>
  <tr><th>Col 1</th><th>Col 2</th><th>Col 3</th></tr>
</thead>
<tfoot>
  <tr><td colspan="3">Footer</td></tr>
</tfoot>
<tbody>
  <tr><td>Cell 1</td><td>Cell 2</td><td>Cell 3</td></tr>
</tbody> </table>

</body>
```

Cell Content Alignment

The position of data within a table cell can be controlled with two attributes provided in HTML 4 for the <td> tag.

Horizontal alignment can be specified with the "align" attribute that may have a value of left, center or right.

If the horizontal alignment is not specified the data will normally be positioned horizontally at the left by default.

Vertical alignment can be specified with the "valign" attribute that may have a value of top, middle or bottom.

If the vertical alignment is not specified the data will normally be positioned vertically in the middle by default.

The example below creates a table illustrating how data alignment can be changed using these attributes:

Specialised attributes and values for data alignment are given in the full specifications. For details see http://www.w3c.org.

```
<body>

<table border="1" cellpadding="3"
       cellspacing="0" width="250">
<tr>
<td align="center" valign="middle">Centre<br>
                                  Middle</td>
<td align="left" valign="top">Top Left</td>
<td align="right" valign="bottom">Bottom Right</td>
</tr>
</table>

</body>
```

Cell Style

Style sheet rules can be applied to table cells and rows using either an id name, or a class, or both id name and class.

The example below applies rules to Cell1 with its id name and to Cell2 using a class name. Cell3 has style rules applied with both id and class.

In the bottom row the font for all cells is specified in the style sheet using the id name of the <tr> tag.

Use a style sheet rule to set the overall background colour of the table and its borders.

```
<!DOCTYPE HTML PUBLIC "-//W3C//DTD HTML 4.01//EN"
            "http://www.w3.org/TR/html4/strict.dtd">
<head> <title>Cell Style</title>
<style type="text/css">
<!--
#cell1 { color:white; background-color:black; }
.silver { text-align:center; background-color:silver; }
#cell3 { font-style:italic; }
#row2 { font-family:monospace; }
//-->
</style> </head> <body>
<table border="1" cellpadding="10" cellspacing="2">
<tr> <td id="cell1">Cell1</td>
    <td class="silver">Cell2</td>
    <td id="cell3" class="silver">Cell3</td> </tr>
<tr id="row2">
  <td>Cell4</td><td>Cell5</td><td>Cell6</td> </tr>
</table> </body>
```

Table Frame and Rules

The appearance of a HTML 4 table can be customized using the "frame" and "rules" attributes of the <table> tag.

Possible values for these attributes are listed in the table below and the example demonstrates them in action:

 By default browsers will normally display all these unless the table border width is set at zero.

Frame	Specifies	Rules	Specifies
above	top side only	groups	display ruled lines between table header, body and footer only
below	bottom side only		
hsides	top and bottom only		
vsides	left and right only	rows	lines between rows
lhs	left-hand side only	cols	lines between columns
rhs	right-hand side only	all	lines between all rows and columns
box	all four sides		

```
<body>

<table border="1" cellpadding="3" cellspacing="2"
width="250" frame="below" rules="cols">
<tr><td>Cell1</td><td>Cell2</td><td>Cell3</td></tr>
<tr><td>Cell4</td><td>Cell5</td><td>Cell6</td></tr>
</table>

</body>
```

Grouping Columns

Table columns may be grouped together so that style rules can be applied to all columns within the group.

The columns are grouped using <colgroup> </colgroup> tags together with their "span" attribute to assign the number of columns to be placed in that group.

In the example below the table has two column groups to which style rules have been applied:

If the span attribute is omitted the <colgroup> is assumed to span one column by default.

```
<!DOCTYPE HTML PUBLIC "-//W3C//DTD HTML 4.01//EN"
            "http://www.w3.org/TR/html4/strict.dtd">
<head> <title>Column Groups</title>
<style type="text/css">
<!--
#group1 { background-color:silver; }
#group2 { color:white; background-color:gray; }
//-->
</style> </head>
<body>
<table border="1" cellpadding="3" cellspacing="2"
width="250">
<colgroup id="group1" span="2"></colgroup>
<colgroup id="group2"></colgroup>
<tr><td>Cell1</td><td>Cell2</td><td>Cell3</td></tr>
<tr><td>Cell4</td><td>Cell5</td><td>Cell6</td></tr>
<tr><td>Cell7</td><td>Cell8</td><td>Cell9</td></tr>
</table> </body>
```

Column Widths

To help the browser lay out a table more quickly all table column widths should be specified at the start of the table.

Column widths are defined, in pixels or as a percentage of overall table width, by the "width" attribute of a <col> tag.

The <col> tag does not have a closing tag.

A "span" attribute in the <col> tag may assign a number of columns to which its width value should apply.

This table uses 100% of total available width (excluding margins) with columns of 25%, 25% and 50% of the total:

 All the <col> tags for a table can optionally be contained inside a set of <colgroup> </colgroup> tags.

```
<!DOCTYPE HTML PUBLIC "-//W3C//DTD HTML 4.01//EN"
            "http://www.w3.org/TR/html4/strict.dtd">
<head> <title>Column Widths</title>
<style type="text/css">
<!--
#col1 { color:white; background-color:gray; }
#col2 { background-color:silver; }
//-->
</style> </head> <body>
<table border="1" cellpadding="3" cellspacing="2"
width="100%">
<col id="col1" span="2" width="25%">
<col id="col2" width="50%">
<tr><td>Cell1</td><td>Cell2</td><td>Cell3</td></tr>
<tr><td>Cell4</td><td>Cell5</td><td>Cell6</td></tr>
</table> </body>
```

Summary Attribute

All <table> tags should include a descriptive summary attribute, like the one in this example, for use by non-visual browsers.

```
<!DOCTYPE HTML PUBLIC "-//W3C//DTD HTML 4.01//EN"
           "http://www.w3.org/TR/html4/strict.dtd">
<head> <title>Sample Table</title>
<meta http-equiv="Content-type"
  content="text/html; charset=ISO-8859-1">
<style type="text/css">
<!--
table { text-align:center; }
th   { background-color:black;color:white; }
td   { background-color:silver; }
//-->
</style> </head> <body>
<table border="0" cellpadding="3" cellspacing="2"
       width="250" summary="Tyre Pressure Conversions">
<caption>Tyre Pressures</caption>
<colgroup><col width="125"><col width="125"></colgroup>
<thead> <tr><th>lb/sq.in</th>
     <th>kg/cm<sup><small>2</small></sup></th> </tr> </thead>
<tbody>
  <tr><td>26</td><td>1.8</td></tr>
  <tr><td>28</td><td>2.0</td></tr>
  <tr><td>30</td><td>2.2</td></tr>
</tbody>
</table> </body>
```

Hyperlinks and Anchors

This chapter explains the special ability of HTML to define hyperlinks that enable users to navigate around the Web. There are examples showing how HTML 4 tags can specify content as an anchor or a hyperlink to a variety of targets.

Covers

Chapter Seven

Creating Hyperlinks

Text or an image in a HTML 4 document body can become a hyperlink "anchor" when contained in <a> </a> tags that specify a destination for that link.

The destination is assigned to an attribute of the <a> tag called "href" and may be an absolute or relative address.

In the browser the hyperlink is displayed in a manner that distinguishes the link from regular document content.

For example, text that is a hyperlink may be displayed as reverse video, different colour or underlined. Images that are hyperlinks are often displayed with a coloured border.

In a Web browser the link destination address will generally be displayed in the windows status bar whenever the user places the pointer over a hyperlink anchor.

The example below illustrates a text hyperlink that will open a destination document when the user follows the link:

The destination may be any type of file that the browser can recognize.

```
<!DOCTYPE HTML PUBLIC "-//W3C//DTD HTML 4.01//EN"
                "http://www.w3.org/TR/html4/strict.dtd">
<head> <title>Page 1</title> </head>
<body>
<p>Click<a href="http://localhost/page2.html">here</a>
to open Page 2.
</p>
</body>
```

Following Links

HTML 4 provides three means to follow hyperlinks:

Pointer
Use a mouse, trackball or similar device to place a screen pointer over the link then click to load the new document.

Tab
Use a Tab key to navigate across the links in a document then hit Enter to load the new document. Typically the tab order follows the order in which links appear on the page.

The accesskey attribute may also be used in <area>, <label>, <textarea>, <input>, <legend> and <button> elements.

Access Key
Use a designated character key to load the new document. The key is specified with the "accesskey" attribute of the <a> element and pressing the key gives focus to the link.

The method of entering the access key will vary according to platform. For instance Windows users must press Alt+access key, and Mac users must press Cmd+access key.

In the example below an access key has been added to the code on the facing page. Entering the access key (Alt+x) will give focus to the link, then hit Enter to load the page.

```
<!DOCTYPE HTML PUBLIC "-//W3C//DTD HTML 4.01//EN"
              "http://www.w3.org/TR/html4/strict.dtd">

<head> <title>Page 1</title> </head>
<body> <p>
<a href="http://localhost/page2.html" accesskey="x">
    Hit access key x</a> to open page 2.
</p> </body>
```

Fragment Anchors

A hyperlink destination can be specified as another point in the current document using fragment anchors.

The fragment anchor is created with the "name" attribute of the <a> tag which is assigned a given name.

Hyperlinks may then use this name preceded by a hash mark as a link destination.

When the user follows a link to a fragment anchor the browser window generally displays the document starting from the point where the anchor is located.

This type of hyperlink is often seen at the end of long documents to provide a return to the top of the page.

In the example below the start of the document creates a fragment anchor and the end of the document provides a hyperlink to jump back to it:

A document may contain innumerable fragment anchors but each name must be unique.

```
<body>
<p> <a name="top_of_page">Welcome</a> </p>

<!-- [long document content ] -->

<p> <a href="#top_of_page">Top of Page</a> </p>

</body>
```

Link to Element

In HTML 4 the "id" attribute of any content tag can be used to specify the destination of a hyperlink.

The tag's id attribute is assigned a given name that can be used with a leading hash mark to specify a link destination.

This name is more correctly called a "fragment identifier" and can be used to navigate around a document in the same way as the example on the opposite page.

A hyperlink can load another document to display in the window at the point where a fragment identifier is located.

In this example a hyperlink in one document opens a second document at the location of a fragment identifier:

```
<head> <title>Page 1</title> <head>
<body>
<p><a href="page2.html#line2">Page 2 - Line 2</a></p>
</body>
```

The entire document is loaded but the window is automatically scrolled down to the location of the fragment identifier.

```
<head> <title>Page 2</title> <head>
<body>
<p id="line1">This is line 1</p>
<p id="line2">This is line 2</p>
<p id="line3">This is line 3</p>
</body>
```

Link Title Tooltip

The "title" attribute of an <a> anchor tag can be useful to provide information about the destination of a hyperlink.

When the user moves the pointer over a hyperlink the browser may display the title attribute value as a tooltip.

```
<body> <p>Add more excitement to your pages -<br>
Learn client-side scripting with<br>
<a href="jsies.gif"
    title="Click here to view the book cover">
JavaScript in easy steps</a> </p> </body>
```

The destination can be any type of recognized file – a GIF file is used here.

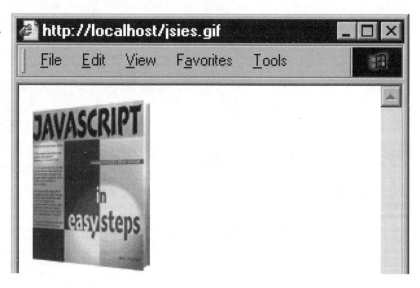

Link to Protocol

Hyperlinks in HTML 4 documents may have a script function as their "destination" rather than a location address.

The link must specify the protocol name followed by a colon then the function name that is to be called.

Most typically this will be a call to a JavaScript function using the protocol specifier "javascript:".

This feature is extremely useful in the creation of interactive Web pages to respond to user actions.

In the following example the hyperlink destination uses a protocol specifier to call a JavaScript function that will display the current date and time in an alert dialog box:

Hyperlinks can also use other recognized protocols for the destination.

```
<body>
<p>
<!-- PopUp Date & Time -->
<a href="javascript:alert( new Date().toGMTString() )">
Click to show current date and time</a>
</p>
</body>
```

Images as Hyperlinks

Images can be used to create a hyperlink in place of regular text by surrounding the image tag with <a> anchor tags.

Most browsers will automatically indicate that the image is a hyperlink by adding a border around the image.

This may look unattractive on a Web page but the image borders can be removed if the style sheet sets their border-width to zero.

The following example displays a text hyperlink and two image hyperlinks where one image is made border-less:

For more on images in HTML 4 documents – see page 88.

```
<head> <title>Image Links</title>
<style type="text/css">
<!--
.noborder { border-width:0; }
//-->
</style><head>
<body>
<p> <a href="page2.html">Click Here</a>
<a href="page2.html">
<img src="click.gif" width="60" height="60" alt="Click">
</a>
<a href="page2.html">
<img src="click.gif" width="60" height="60" alt="Click"
class="noborder"></a> </p>
</body>
```

Image Map Hyperlinks

A single image can have multiple hyperlink destinations if an image map is added to define distinct areas for each link.

To add an image map the image tag must assign the map name preceded by a hash mark to its "usemap" attribute.

The map is contained within <map> </map> tags which have a "name" attribute to specify a given name for the map.

Each distinct area of the image that is to become a hyperlink is defined within the maps <area> tags that state the coordinates of the area, its shape and link destination.

This example uses one image map to create three hyperlinks:

Notice that the active border surrounds the whole image – not each link.

```
<body> <p>
<img src="trio.gif" usemap="#trio" alt="Trio Image">
<map name="trio">
<area shape="circle" coords="62,21,18" href="p1.html"
alt="Link to page 1">
<area shape="circle" coords="28,79,18" href="p2.html"
alt="Link to page 2">
<area shape="circle" coords="97,79,18" href="p3.html"
alt="Link to page 3">
</map>
</p> </body>
```

Hyperlinks can be used to call script functions – see page 83.

Mapping Coordinates

The "shape" attribute of an <area> tag can define an image area as either "circle" ,"rect" (rectangle) or "poly" (polygon).

Coordinate values assigned to the "coords" attribute in the <area> tag will vary according to the shape specified.

The table below lists the coordinates required by each shape:

The image map example on the previous page uses the circle shape to create the hyperlink "hotspots".

Shape	Coordinates
rect	left-x, top-y, right-x, bottom-y
circle	center-x, center-y, radius
poly	x1, y1, x2, y2, x3, y3,etc - one pair for each point. The first point and the final point must have identical coordinates to join up the shape

Calculating coordinates manually can be a difficult task. Fortunately modern graphics programs like Photoshop and Paint Shop Pro 7 are able to generate image map code that can simply be pasted into the appropriate HTML document.

There are also inexpensive image mapping applications available such as the CoffeeCup image mapper shown here:

Find out more about the CoffeeCup image mapper on the Web at http://www.coffeecup.com.

Embedding Contents

This chapter demonstrates how to create a content-rich page by adding diverse content into a HTML 4 document. There are examples that incorporate other text and HTML documents plus images, applets, animation and video.

Covers

Chapter Eight

Add an Image

The HTML 4 <img> tag can be used to add images to the content of a document body.

An <img> image element does not have a closing tag.

There are however a number of attributes that must be supplied inside an <img> tag for it to be valid.

The image file location may be assigned to the "src" attribute as either a relative or absolute address.

A "src" attribute should be assigned the address of the image to be displayed and an "alt" attribute must specify a text alternative in case the browser cannot display the image.

The dimensions to display the image must be assigned to the respective "width" and "height" attributes. These do not need to be the actual image dimensions as the browser will resize an image to suit the specified size.

In order for a script to reference an image it is important to assign a name to the image with the <img> "id" attribute.

The following example demonstrates an image tag called "pic1" with correctly specified attributes:

```
<!DOCTYPE HTML PUBLIC "-//W3C//DTD HTML 4.01//EN"
          "http://www.w3.org/TR/html4/strict.dtd">
<head> <title>Image Tags</title> </head>
<body>
<p><img id="pic1" src="fun.gif"
     width="200" height="75" alt="HTML 4 is Fun"></p>
</body>
```

Images with Maps

A map can be specified with the "usemap" attribute of the <img> tag to react to the user of a HTML 4 document.

The example below assigns lines of script to "onmouseout" and "onmouseover" attributes that display simple messages:

If the image uses a map all the <area> tags must also have "alt" attributes to specify alternative text.

```
<head> <title>Image With Map</title> </head>

<body>
<p>
<img id="pic1" src="areas.gif" width="200"
            height="50" alt="Areas" usemap="#nums">
<map name="nums">
<area shape="rect" coords="0,0,100,50" alt="Area 1"
onmouseout="document.f.txt.value=''" href="a1.html"
onmouseover="document.f.txt.value='Area 1'">

<area shape="rect" coords="100,0,200,50" alt="Area 2"
onmouseout="document.f.txt.value=''" href="a2.html"
onmouseover="document.f.txt.value='Area 2'">
</map> </p>

<form name="f" action="">
<p> <input name="txt" type="text" value=""> </p>
</form>

</body>
```

Form elements are covered in detail later – see chapter 10.

Objects and Mime Types

HTML 4 introduces the <object> </object> tags as a means to embed resources into a HTML document.

The <object> tag may use its "width" and "height" attributes to specify the display dimensions of the resource.

Most importantly its "data" attribute will specify the object location and its "type" attribute will describe a MIME type.

A Multipurpose Internet Mail Extension (MIME) is a registered description of a resource that can be universally recognised by all Web browsers.

The table below lists some of the MIME types that are most frequently used to describe common resources:

For details of all the many MIME types – see the W3C Web site online at http://www.w3c.org.

MIME Type	Object Type
image/gif	GIF image resource
image/jpeg	JPG, JPEG, JPEimage resource
image/png	PNG image resource
text/plain	TXT regular text document
text/html	HTM, HTML markup text documents
text/css	CSS cascading style sheet
text/javascript	JS javascript script resource
audio/x-wav	WAV sound resource
audio/x-mpeg	MP3 music resource
video/mpeg	MPEG, MPG, MPE video resource
video/x-msvideo	AVI video resource
application/java	CLASS java resource
application/pdf	PDF portable document

Embed an Image Object

The <object> </object> tags enable all kinds of content to become embedded into a HTML 4 document.

The location of the data to be embedded is assigned to an <object> attribute called "data" and the "type" attribute is assigned its MIME type.

An alternative text description can be contained between the tags to be displayed if the object cannot be embedded.

This example attempts to embeds a GIF image into a HTML 4 document and the browser screenshots illustrate the result of both failure and success:

All alternative content between the <object> tags is ignored unless the object is not embedded.

```
<head> <title>Embedded Image Object</title> </head>

<body>
<p>
<object data="lilguy.gif" type="image/gif" width="29"
height="24">[Lilguy Image]<br> </object>
This is an embedded image object.
</p>

</body>
```

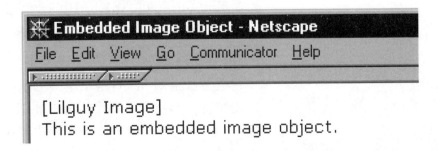

Embed a Text File Object

A plain text file can be embedded into a HTML 4 document with <object> tags in the same way as embedded images.

Here the MIME type is specified as "text/plain" and the alternative text provides a hyperlink to the text file:

```
<head> <title>Embedded Text File Object</title> </head>
<body>
<p> This is text in the main document that<br>
<object id="obj1" data="text.txt" type="text/plain"
width="250" height="70">
[Click <a href="text.txt">here</a> for details]
</object>
<br>continues around embedded objects. </p>
</body>
```

Notice that the displayed text retains the line break from the original file.

Embed a HTML Object

HTML 4 documents can embed other HTML files by using <object> tags together with the MIME type of "text/html".

This example usefully demonstrates how to embed another HTML document from a remote location:

```
<head> <title>Embedded HTML Object</title> </head>
<body>
<p>This is text in the main document that <br>
<object data="content.html" type="text/html" width="255"
height="80">
[Click <a href="http://fardomain/content.html">here </a>
for more details] </object>
<br>continues around the inline frame.</p>
</body>
```

Note that the embedded object area automatically has a scroll bar.

Embed a Java Applet

An <object> tag attribute called "classid" can be used to embed a Java applet into a HTML document.

The "classid" attribute is assigned the "java:" protocol specifier followed by the name of the Java class.

As usual the "data" attribute specifies the file location.

When "classid" is used the regular "type" attribute should be replaced by a "codetype" attribute to specify the MIME type.

In the example below the Java class file called "hello.class" is assigned to the "classid" attribute, without its file extension.

Also the "codetype" attribute identifies the MIME type to the browser as a Java applet:

The default text between the <object> tags is only to be displayed when the applet cannot be run.

```
<body>

<p>This is text in the main document that
<br>
<object id="applet1" classid="java:hello"
        data="../javafiles/hello.class"
        codetype="application/java"
        height="50" width="250">[Java Applet]</object>

<br>continues around embedded objects.
</p>

</body>
```

Add Applet Parameters

Java applets that have variable parameters may have their initial values set with the HTML 4 <param> tag.

This tag does not have an associated closing tag and all the <param> tags are contained in the applet's <object> tags.

Parameter names that are recognized by the Java code can be assigned to the <param> "name" attribute. Then its "value" attribute can specify an initial value for use by the Java code.

This example sets some initial applet colour parameters:

The specified colours here are hexadecimal for silver, white and black.

```
<body>
<p>This is text in the main document that<br>
<object id="applet2" width="250 "height="130"
        classid="java:clock" codetype="application/java">
<param name="bgcolor" value="C0C0C0">
<param name="fgcolor1" value="FFFFFF">
<param name="fgcolor2" value="000000">[clock]</object>
<br>continues around embedded objects.
</p>
</body>
```

Embedding Multimedia

The HTML 4 <object> </object> tags allow for all types of multimedia resources to be embedded in a document.

Browsers determine if they can directly render an embedded multimedia resource or if they can call upon a helper application to do so.

This example embeds a video into a HTML document which the browser calls upon a helper application to run:

```
<body>
<p>This is text in the main document that
<br>
<object id="obj1" data="movie.mpg" type="video/mpeg">
      [video]<br></object>
<br>continues around embedded objects.
</p>
</body>
```

Providing Object Options

The browser can be given a selection of object options by nesting the HTML 4 <object> </object> tags.

This can provide a descending choice of object options for the browser to use according to its capabilities.

The following example builds on the previous example to provide a still image option if the video cannot be run:

The default text option will be displayed in the event that both video and still image cannot be displayed

```
<head> <title>Embedded Video Object</title> </head>

<body>
<p>This is text in the main document that <br>

<object id="obj1" data="movie.mpg" type="video/mpeg">
  <object id="obj2" data="movie.gif" type="image.gif">
    [Click <a href="movie.html">here</a> for details]
  </object>
</object>

<br>continues around embedded objects.

</p>
</body>
```

ActiveX Sound

Microsoft ActiveX components can be embedded in HTML 4 documents to provide excellent multimedia controls for the Internet Explorer Web browser.

Set "autoStart" to "true" and "playCount" to "2" to play a sound file twice when the document loads

The ActiveX component is embedded using <object> tags and must assign the Microsoft "clsid" reference to its "classid" attribute.

Initial values are set with <param> tags to specify the file location, autostart and loop parameters.

This example plays the specified file just once when the user pushes the play button on the ActiveX control panel:

```
<head> <title>Embedded Audio Player</title> </head>
<body>
<p>This is text in the main document that<br>

<object id="Player1" width="250" height="65"
    classid="clsid:6BF52A52-394A-11d3-B153-00C04F79FAA6">
  <param name="URL" value="music.mp3">
  <param name="autoStart" value="false">
  <param name="playCount" value="1">
</object>

<br>continues around embedded objects.</p>
</body>
```

Set the "width" and "height" attributes to zero to hide the control panel.

ActiveX Video

The same ActiveX control shown opposite can also be used to play neatly embedded videos as seen in this example:

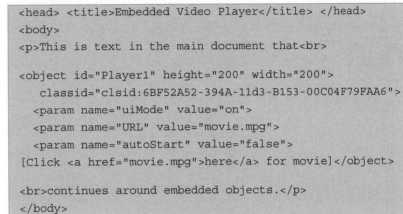

```
<head> <title>Embedded Video Player</title> </head>
<body>
<p>This is text in the main document that<br>

<object id="Player1" height="200" width="200">
    classid="clsid:6BF52A52-394A-11d3-B153-00C04F79FAA6">
  <param name="uiMode" value="on">
  <param name="URL" value="movie.mpg">
  <param name="autoStart" value="false">
[Click <a href="movie.mpg">here</a> for movie]</object>

<br>continues around embedded objects.</p>
</body>
```

Notice the "uiMode" parameter that alters controls – values can be "none", "mini" or "full".

ActiveX Flash Movie

The <object> tags are used to embed Macromedia Flash movies in HTML 4 documents by assigning the Flash ActiveX control to the "classid" attribute, as seen here:

To find out more about Flash see the "Flash 5 in easy steps" book in this series.

```
<head> <title>Embedded Flash Movie</title> </head>
<body>
<p>This is text in the main document that<br>
<object id="rollers" width="250" height="207"
    classid="clsid:D27CDB6E-AE6D-11cf-96B8-444553540000">
<param name="movie" value="rollers.swf">
<param name="quality" value="high">
<param name="bgcolor" value="#ffffff">
</object>
<br>continues around embedded objects.</p>
</body>
```

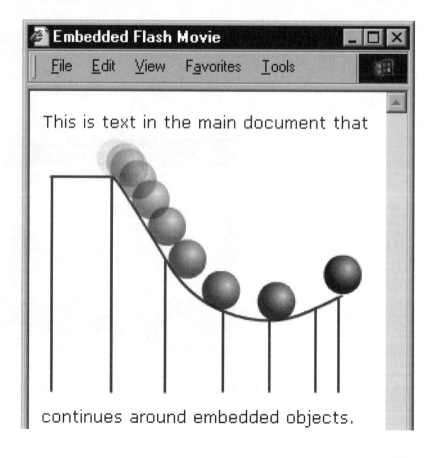

Using Frames

This chapter demonstrates how to use HTML 4 to create multi-document pages with frames. There are examples that illustrate control of the frames' appearance to define how the whole page should appear in a Web browser.

Covers

Chapter Nine

The Frameholder Document

Frames provide a way to display multiple HTML documents in a single browser window.

This means that some documents can remain on display while others in a different frame are changed.

Typically a window might have three frames consisting of a top banner frame, a left-side menu frame and a main frame containing the changing page content.

The frames could occupy the window like this:

This frame arrangement is demonstrated on page 105.

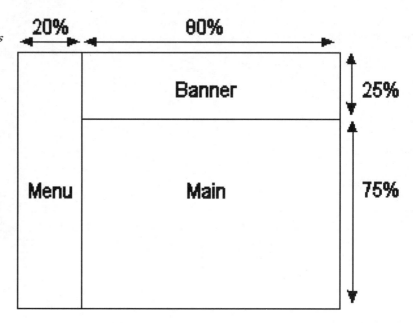

The arrangement of the frames is controlled by the HTML 4 <frameset> </frameset> tags in a dedicated frameholder HTML document.

Frameholder documents consist of a <head> section and a <frameset> section and must start with this special DTD:

```
<!DOCTYPE HTML PUBLIC
"-//W3C//DTD HTML 4.01 Frameset//EN"
"http://www.w3.org/TR/html4/frameset.dtd">
```

Two-Column Frameset

The HTML 4 <frameset> </frameset> tags control the horizontal allocation of frame width with a "cols" attribute.

Values assigned to the "cols" attribute may be expressed either as pixels or as a percentage where total width is 100%.

The frame values are assigned to the "cols" attribute from left to right as a comma-delimited list.

Alternatively a wildcard value can be assigned with a "★". This is most useful when the other frames are assigned set pixel values to mean "the available remaining width".

The <frameset> tags contain <frame> tags that specify the location of each frame document with their "src" attribute.

This example frameholder document arranges the window to display two frames as 20% and 80% of total available width:

The <frame> tag does not have any closing tag.

```
<!DOCTYPE HTML PUBLIC
"-//W3C//DTD HTML 4.01 Frameset//EN"
"http://www.w3.org/TR/html4/frameset.dtd">

<head> <title>Two Column Frameset</title> </head>

<frameset cols="20%,80%">

  <frame src="menu.html">

  <frame src="main.html">

</frameset>
```

Two-Row Frameset

The HTML 4 <frameset> </frameset> tags control the vertical allocation of frame height with a "rows" attribute.

Values assigned to the "rows" attribute may be expressed either as pixels or as a percentage where total height is 100%.

The frame values are assigned to the "rows" attribute from left to right as a comma-delimited list.

Alternatively a wildcard value can be assigned with a "★". This is most useful when the other frames are assigned set pixel values to mean "the available remaining height".

This example frameholder document arranges the window to display two frames as 25% and 75% of total available height:

Note that this frameset arrangement could have used the wildcard as:

rows="25%,"*

or (equally):

*rows=" *,75%"*

```
<!DOCTYPE HTML PUBLIC
"-//W3C//DTD HTML 4.01 Frameset//EN"
"http://www.w3.org/TR/html4/frameset.dtd">
<head> <title>Two Row Frameset</title> </head>
<frameset cols="25%,75%">
   <frame src="banner.html">
   <frame src="main.html">
</frameset>
```

Nested Frameset

Frameholder documents can contain nested framesets to provide a more elaborate arrangement of frames.

An initial <frameset> could, for instance, assign column widths to two frames. The second <frame> could be replaced with a nested <frameset> that might then assign row heights to two frames.

This arrangement is illustrated in the example below that creates a window containing a total of three frames:

This example combines the previous two examples and follows the frame layout on page 102.

```
<!DOCTYPE HTML PUBLIC
"-//W3C//DTD HTML 4.01 Frameset//EN"
"http://www.w3.org/TR/html4/frameset.dtd">
<head> <title>Nested Frameset</title> </head>

<frameset cols="20%,80%">
  <frame src="menu.html">
  <frameset rows="25%,75%">
    <frame src="banner.html">
    <frame src="main.html">
  </frameset>
</frameset>
```

Frame Appearance

If a border is not required between frames set the <frame> "frameborder" attribute to zero. If scroll bars are not required assign a value of "no" to its "scrolling" attribute.

Positioning of the frames contents from the frames edges can be specified by assigning positive pixel values to the <frame> attributes "marginwidth" and "marginheight".

A frames dimension can be made permanent by adding the single-word attribute "noresize" into its <frame> tag.

This example removes all frame borders and the banner-frame scrollbars from the example on the previous page:

Although not compliant with the HTML 4 specifications, browser issues make it necessary to add 'border="0"' in the first <frameset> to hide borders.

```
<!DOCTYPE HTML PUBLIC "-//W3C//DTD HTML 4.01 Frameset//
EN" "http://www.w3.org/TR/html4/frameset.dtd">
<head> <title>Nested Frameset</title> </head>
<frameset cols="20%,80%" border="0">
<frame src="menu.html" frameborder="0">
<frameset rows="25%,75%">
<frame src="banner.html" frameborder="0" scrolling="no">
<frame src="main.html" frameborder="0">
</frameset> </frameset
```

Frame Targets

Hyperlinks, in any frame, treat the frame as a separate window and will load new location pages in that same frame.

Previously a "target" attribute could be used inside <a> elements to specify which frame should load a new page.

This attribute has not been included in the Strict HTML 4 specifications in order to discourage the use of frames.

Future browser devices may not be able to display framed documents.

Scripting may be used to specify which frame should load new location pages – so hyperlinks in a Menu frame could load new documents into a Main frame.

This example illustrates the normal method of loading:

```
<!DOCTYPE HTML PUBLIC "-//W3C//DTD HTML 4.01//EN"
              "http://www.w3.org/TR/html4/strict.dtd">
<head> <title>Main Frame</title> </head>

<body>
<p>Main<br>
<a href="newpage.html">Click for new page</a>
</p> </body>>
```

Alternative Content

Using framed windows to display multiple documents is considered to be bad practice by many people. As the diversity of browsers increases it may be that framed windows are made obsolete.

In order to accommodate browsers that cannot display frames, or that have the frame facility disabled by user preferences, it is a good idea to provide an alternative.

The HTML 4 <noframes> </noframes> tags can be used in a frameholder document to contain content that will be displayed when the frames cannot be loaded.

In the example below the <noframes> tags provide a notice explaining why the page did not load and offer a hyperlink to visit an alternative unframed page:

The W3C may have separated the frameset document with the intention of making frames obsolete at some point in the future.

```
<!DOCTYPE HTML PUBLIC
"-//W3C//DTD HTML 4.01 Frameset//EN"
"http://www.w3.org/TR/html4/frameset.dtd">
<head> <title>Nested Frameset</title> </head>
<frameset cols="20%,80%" border="0">
  <frame name="menu" src="menu.html" frameborder="0">
  <frameset rows="25%,75%">
    <frame name="banner" src="banner.html"
           frameborder="0" scrolling="no">
    <frame name="main" src="main.html" frameborder="0">
  </frameset>

<noframes>This page uses frames.<br>
Click <a href="noframepage.html">here</a> for a
frameless version of the page</a> </noframes></frameset>
```

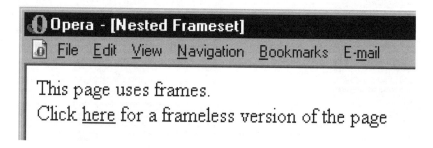

Creating Forms

This chapter illustrates how HTML 4 forms can submit data to a Web server. Each type of form element that can interact with the user is demonstrated by example.

Covers

Chapter Ten

A Simple Form

A form is a section of a HTML 4 document body that can contain regular content together with a number of "controls" which may be modified by the user.

Typical controls include text inputs and radio buttons.

The modified form can be submitted to the server where the forms control input will be processed.

All form content is contained in <form> </form> tags.

The <form> tag must have an "action" attribute that specifies the location of a form handler to process the form data when the form is submitted to the server.

Often the form handler will be a CGI script like the address assigned to the "action" attribute in this simple form:

A form must also provide a means for the user to submit the form data.

```
<body>
<form action="http://domain/formhandler.cgi">
<p>
First name: <input type="text" name="firstname"> <br>
Last name: <input type="text" name="lastname"> <br>
<input type="radio" name="sex" value="Male">Male
<input type="radio" name="sex" value="Female">Female
<input type="submit" value="Submit">
</p>
</form>
</body>
```

Submission Information

The HTML 4 <form> tag has several attributes that may be used to provide information regarding form submission.

 For more on form-handling with CGI scripts see "CGI & Perl in easy steps".

An attribute named "method" can specify the type of form submission as either "get" or "post". If unspecified the default method is "get" although "post" is preferred for submissions to CGI script form handlers.

Each form will automatically submit its data in an encoded format that is acceptable to the server. This default MIME type is "application/x-www-form-urlencoded".

Optionally the encoding type can be specified manually with a <form> attribute called "enctype".

For instance the "enctype" attribute may specify a MIME type to indicate the submission of another file by assigning a value of "multipart/form-data".

Alternatively submissions in plain text format might assign a MIME type of "text/plain" to the "enctype" attribute.

Most forms however will use the default encoding so the "enctype" need not be set manually.

All forms should be named by assigning a unique name to the "name" attribute in the <form> tag. The given name can then be used by scripts to refer to the form.

The opening <form> tag on the opposite page could be amended to name the form as "myform" and because it is a submission to a CGI script the "post" method is specified:

```
<form name="myform"
    action="http://domain/formhandler.cgi"
    method="post">
```

It is important to understand that all form submissions consist of name/value pairs, so the form handler will receive a name together with an associated value.

All the controls in a HTML 4 form must therefore contain a name and value attribute to submit to the form handler.

Text Inputs

Many form controls use a HTML 4 <input> tag with a "type" attribute that specifies the type of that control.

The <input> tag does not have any closing tag.

One of the most common controls is the text input that is created with an <input> tag and an assigned type of "text".

To make the text input useful to a form handler it must also have a name and a value. These are assigned to the <input> "name" and "value" attributes for submission by the form.

Optionally the width of a text input can be specified by assigning an integer to a "size" attribute of the <input> tag.

The example below creates a text input called "txt1" with a width of "12" and an initial value of "Enter".

A user can change this initial value and the form will submit the input name and its final value as a name/value pair:

The width of the text input will be set by the browser's interpretation of the "size" attribute value.

```
<body>
<form name="myform" method="post"
    action="http://domain/formhandler.cgi">
<p>
<input name="txt1" type="text" value="Enter" size="12">
<input type="submit" value="Submit Form">
</p>
</form>
</body>
```

Add "onfocus", "onselect" or "onblur" attributes to call a script from an active text input.

Password Inputs

A user can enter an unlimited number of characters into a text input unless a limit is set with a "maxlength" attribute.

An <input> tags "maxlength" attribute specifies a maximum number of characters that can be entered into an input field.

This may also be used with the "password" type of <input> which is simply a variation of the regular text input.

The only difference is that the password input field displays an asterisk in place of each actual character of the text content, to safeguard against a password being easily visible.

All other attributes that are used in the text input can be used by a password input.

When a form is submitted the password inputs name and actual character content are sent to the form handler.

The example below sets no initial <input> value but limits the maximum permitted entry length to 6 characters:

A script could advise the user when the maximum entry length had been exceeded.

```
<body>
<form name="myform" method="post"
    action="http://domain/formhandler.cgi">
<p>Enter Password [Max.6] <br>
<input name="pwd1" type="password" maxlength="6">
<input type="submit" value="Submit">
</p>
</form>
</body>
```

Checkboxes

A "checkbox" type input is a HTML 4 form control which the user can choose to select or ignore.

If a checkbox has been selected its name and associated value will be sent to the form handler when the form is submitted.

Normally each checkbox will be given a unique name but checkboxes may share a common name to apply multiple values to the same property.

This example below applies two values to the "chk1" property and the CGI script outputs all name/value data:

The CGI script does not receive any data for "chk2" because that checkbox is not selected.

```
<body>
<form name="myform" method="post"
    action="http://localhost/cgi-bin/showall.cgi">
<p>
<input name="chk1" value="coffee" type="checkbox">Coffee
<input name="chk1" value="cream" type="checkbox">Cream
<input name="chk2" value="sugar" type="checkbox">Sugar
<input type="submit" value="Submit">
</p>
</form>
</body>
```

Add the single word "checked" into the input tag to set the initial selection.

Radio Buttons

A "radio" type input is normally one of a group of radio buttons that share a common name. Unlike checkboxes, only one button in the group can be selected at any given time.

When the form is submitted the radio buttons name will be sent together with the value of the selected button.

A radio button group must always have one button selected.

The button to be initially selected can be specified by adding the single word "checked" into its <input> tag.

This example submits the selected button name/value to the CGI script form handler which outputs the data received:

The name and value of the initially selected radio button will always be submitted unless the user selects a different button.

```
<body>
<form name="myform" method="post"
    action="http://localhost/cgi-bin/showall.cgi">
<p>
<input name="Pop" value="Lemon" type="radio">Lemonade
<input name="Pop" value="Cola" type="radio" checked>Cola
<input name="Pop" value="Orange" type="radio">Orangeade
<input type="submit" value="Submit">
</p>
</form>
</body>
```

File Inputs

A "file" type input may select a file for upload with the creation of a special form control.

A default file name can be specified with the "value" attribute of the <input> tag.

Also the control includes a browse facility that allows the user to select an alternative file from a selection dialog.

When the file is selected its path is displayed in a text field which can also be used to type the path of a chosen file.

Using this type of input the <form> tag should specify the MIME type as "multipart/form-data" with its "enctype" attribute to denote that the submission includes a file.

This example creates a file selection input and illustrates a user-selected file ready for submission to the server:

The browser may not display the initial file value in the text field.

```
<body>
<form name="myform" enctype="multipart/formdata"
    method="post" action="http://domain/sortfile.cgi">
<p>
Please select a file for upload...<br>
<input name="fselect" type="file" value="C:/file.java">
<input type="submit" value="Click To Upload">
</p>
</form>
</body>
```

Hidden Inputs

A "hidden" type input does not create any visible form control but is used to store data for submission.

This is particularly useful for scripts to maintain user data when generating a HTML document.

When the form is subsequently submitted the original user data is again sent to the server.

The example below with a readonly "text" type input plus a "hidden" type input will submit both name/value pairs:

Add the word "readonly" to text inputs to prevent the user changing the value of the text field.

```
<body>
<form name="myform" method="post"
    action="http://localhost/cgi-bin/showall.cgi">
<p>
<input name="txt1" type="text" value="Look no hands"
readonly>
<input name="hid1" type="hidden" value="Hidden Hands">
<input type="submit" value="Submit">
</p>
</form>
</body>
```

Push Buttons

The "button" type of <input> creates a push button control that is typically used to run a script function.

A button should have a name and value but neither of these are generally used when the form is submitted to the server.

Whatever is assigned to the <input> tags "value" attribute will be displayed on the button face as its label.

It is the <input> tags "onclick" attribute that is used to execute a script function when the user pushes that button.

The script function will often be contained in a script block within the document head section or in a linked script file.

In the example below some script code is assigned "in-line" to the "onclick" attribute to run when the button is pushed.

This code assigns the browser name to a text input value:

Script functions will not run if the browser does not support the scripting language or it is disabled in user preferences.

```
<body>
<form name="myform" method="post"
      action="http://localhost/cgi-bin/showall.cgi">
<p>
<input name="txt1" type="text" size="28"> <br>
<input name="btn1" type="button" value="Show Browser"
onclick="this.form.txt1.value=navigator.appName">

<input type="submit" value="Submit">
</p>
</form>
</body>
```

Reset Buttons

A reset button can be added to a form to allow the user to return all the form values to their original state.

The reset button is created by assigning "reset" to the <input> tags "type" attribute.

In this example the reset button returns the text input value to its initial value of an empty string:

An "onreset" attribute can be added to the <form> tag to run a script whenever a form is reset.

```
<body>
<form name="myform" method="post"
    action="http://localhost/cgi-bin/showall.cgi">
<p>
<input name="txt1" type="text" size="28" value="">
<br>
<input name="rst1" type="reset" value="Reset">
<input type="submit" value="Submit">
</p>
</form>
</body>
```

Submit Buttons

The "submit" type of input creates a submit button that the user can push to send the form data to the server.

The form's control names and values are typically submitted to a CGI script form handler as name/value pairs.

An "onsubmit" attribute can be added to the <form> tag to assign a script that will run when the form is submitted.

The script will be executed immediately before the form is submitted so the script can make any last minute checks.

This example uses the "onsubmit" attribute to round down floating point values to whole integers in the text input:

A single form may contain multiple submit buttons.

```
<body>
<form name="myform" method="post"
action="http://localhost/cgi-bin/showall.cgi"
onsubmit="myform.txt1.value=Math.floor(myform.txt1.value)">
<p>
<input name="txt1" type="text" value="3.142">
<input type="submit" value="Submit">
</p>
</form>
</body>
```

Image Submit Button

The "image" input type can create a graphical submit button.

This also requires a "src" attribute to specify the location of the button image and an "alt" attribute to specify alternative text for browsers that do not display images.

When the form is submitted the x and y coordinates where the image was clicked are also sent to the server as seen here:

The submitted coordinates are the position across the image – not the position across the page.

```
<body>
<form name="myform" method="post"
    action="http://localhost/cgi-bin/showall.cgi">
<p>
<input name="txt1" type="text" value="HTML 4 is Fun">
<input type="image" src="send.gif" alt="Submit Button">
</p>
</form>
</body>
```

Buttons with Graphics

The HTML 4 <button> </button> tags provide another way to feature a push button in a document.

The content between the tags is displayed on the button face and can include a mixture of text and images.

This example illustrates how the <button> tags can be used to make attractive submit, reset and button types:

These buttons work just like buttons created with <input> but can add images onto the button face.

```
<body>
<form name="myform" method="post"
    action="http://localhost/cgi-bin/showall.cgi">
<p>
<button name="btn1" value="hi" type="button"
        onclick="alert('Hi!')">
<img src="lilguy.gif" alt="Hi">Welcome</button>
</p> <hr> <p>

<button name="btn2" value="submit" type="submit">
<img src="submit.gif" alt="Submit">Submit</button>
 
<button name="btn3" type="reset">
<img src="reset.gif" alt="Reset">Cancel</button>
</p>
</form>
</body>
```

This tag is not implemented in Netscape browsers earlier than version 6.

Using Labels

Text can be associated with a form control by adding the HTML 4 <label> </label> tags to the document.

This tag can have a "for" attribute to assign a controls identity or may surround the control and the associated text.

This example uses both methods to illustrate how the label text can be emphasised with a style sheet rule:

Using the second method <label> tags should only surround the text and a single control.

```
<head> <title>Labels</title>
<style type="text/css">
label {background-color:gray;color:white;}
</style>
</head>
<body>
<form name="myform" method="post"
    action="http://localhost/cgi-bin/showall.cgi">
<p>Please
<label for="colour">enter a colour</label> of choice
<br> <input name="colour" type="text" id="colour">
<br>then
<label>
enter a size<br><input type="text" name="size">
</label>
<input type="submit" value="Submit">
</p>
</form>
</body>
```

Text Areas

The HTML 4 <textarea> </textarea> tags are used to create multi-line text input fields in HTML documents.

They must always contain both "rows" and "cols" attributes to specify the width and height of the text input field.

Also a "name" attribute will be assigned a given name.

Unlike a regular text input a <textarea> has no "value" attribute . Instead it takes any text content between its tags to be its associated value, as seen in the example below:

Text areas will automatically have a scroll bar to accommodate long content.

```
<body>
<form name="myform" method="post"
    action="http://localhost/cgi-bin/showall.cgi">
<p>
<textarea name="tar1" rows="3" cols="25">
You may change the text in this area.</textarea>
<input type="submit" value="Submit">
</p>
</form>
</body>
```

Tab Order

A tab key can be used to navigate through the hyperlinks and form controls in a HTML document, normally following the order in which they appear in the document.

A special tab order can be determined by adding a "tabindex" attribute to any of the tags <a>, <area>, <button>, <input>, <object>, <select> or <textarea>.

These are assigned unique integer values to set the tab order.

Any of the form controls in the above list of tags can be disabled by adding the single word "disabled" into its tag.

Disabled form controls cannot receive input, are not submitted with the form and are ignored in the tab order.

This example has a special tab order and a disabled control:

 Controls that are disabled may appear "greyed-out" in some browsers.

```
<body>
<form name="myform" method="post"
      action="http://localhost/cgi-bin/showall.cgi">
<p>
<input type="text" size="1" tabindex="5">
<input type="text" size="1" tabindex="4" disabled>
<input type="text" size="1" tabindex="2">
<input type="text" size="1" tabindex="2">
<input type="submit" value="Submit" tabindex="1">
</p>
</form>
</body>
```

Selection Menus

The HTML 4 <select> </select> tags create a selection menu from which the user may select a listed option.

The <select> tags should assign a given name to a "name" attribute and should surround the list of options.

Text describing each option is contained between <option> </option> tags and each one must have a "value" attribute.

When the form is submitted the <select> name and the <option> value make up the submitted name/value pair.

The select menu generally appears as a drop-down list unless a "size" attribute is added to the <select> tag to set a height.

The example below illustrates a selection menu and adds the single word "selected" to initially select one of the options:

Add size="3" to this <select> tag to make the menu fixed.

```
<body>
<form name="myform" method="post"
    action="http://localhost/cgi-bin/showall.cgi"> <p>
<select name="myselect">
<option value="1st">First Choice</option>
<option value="2nd" selected>Second Choice</option>
<option value="3rd">Third Choice</option>
</select>
<input type="submit" value="Submit"> </p>
</form>
</body>
```

Add an "onchange" attribute in the <select> tag to call a script function upon selection.

Grouping Menus

Select menu options may be grouped together with the HTML 4 <optgroup> </optgroup> tags.

A name for each group can be assigned to a "label" attribute inside its <optgroup> tag.

The example below displays the name given to each option group in the fixed-height select menu:

Browsers that do not support <optgroup> will still display the select menu — without the group labels.

```
<body>
<form name="myform" method="post"
    action="http://localhost/cgi-bin/showall.cgi">
<p>
<select name="myselect" size="6">
<optgroup label="Group 1">
<option value="1st">First Choice</option>
<option value="2nd">Second Choice</option>
</optgroup>
<optgroup label="Group 2">
<option value="1st">First Choice</option>
<option value="2nd">Second Choice</option>
</optgroup>
</select>
<input type="submit" value="Submit">
</p>
</form>
</body>
```

Grouping Form Fields

Associated form input fields can be grouped into "fieldsets" which the browser may display in a manner that makes their association apparent to the user.

The <fieldset> </fieldset> tags are used to contain the associated inputs. The fieldset may also display a group name defined between <legend> </legend> tags.

This example illustrates two fieldsets and legends:

Browsers may display fieldsets in a variety of different ways.

```
<body>
<form name="myform" method="post"
   action="http://localhost/cgi-bin/showall.cgi">
<fieldset> <legend>Select Colour</legend>
<input type="radio" name="colr" value="red" checked>Red
<input type="radio" name="colr" value="grn">Green
<input type="radio" name="colr" value="blu">Blue
</fieldset>
<fieldset> <legend>Select Size</legend>
<input type="radio" name="size" value="s">Small
<input type="radio" name="size" value="m">Medium
<input type="radio" name="size" value="l" checked>Large
</fieldset>
<p> <input type="submit" value="Submit"> </p>
</form>
</body>
```

Borders and Margins

This chapter explains the components comprising blocks of HTML document content. Examples demonstrate how style rules can be used to manipulate each component.

Covers

Chapter Eleven

The Content Box

Each block of document content is placed onto the page in an invisible content box.

The content box has three properties that may optionally specify how the block of content appears.

Content box properties have a top, bottom, left and right part that can be addressed individually.

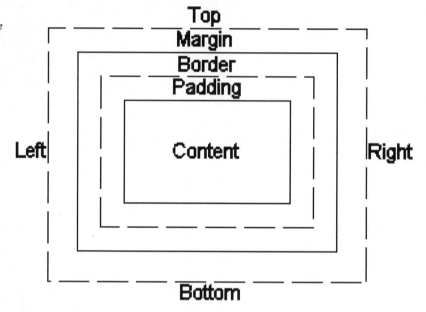

A "padding" property defines the edges of the content box. With a padding width of zero the content box edges are identical to the contained content edges. The content box edges extend as the padding width is increased.

A "border" property defines the width of the area immediately surrounding the content box. With a border width of zero the border edges remain identical to the content box edges. The border edges extend as the border width is increased.

A "margin" property defines the width of the area that immediately surrounds the border edges. With a margin width of zero the margin edges remain identical to the border edges. The margin edges extend as the margin width is increased.

Background and Border Colour

To create a border around a block of content it is necessary to specify its border properties for colour, width and style.

The style sheet "border-color" property will specify the colour of the entire content box border.

Similarly its width can be specified with a "border-width" property and style of border with a "border-style" property.

The example below initially sets all content box borders to black with a width of 25 pixels and drawn in a solid style.

A "background-color" property is assigned a recognised colour name to set a background colour for the content box.

Top and bottom borders are assigned individual colours that supersede the general border colour for just those borders.

Individual border colours could have also been set using the properties "border-left-color" and "border-right-color".

```
<head> <title>Background &amp; Border Colour</title>
<style type="text/css">
<!--
p {border-color:black; border-width:25px;
      border-style:solid;
      background-color:silver;
      border-top-color:gray; border-bottom-color:gray; }
//-->
</style>
</head>

<body><p>Content</p></body>
```

Remember to set a width and style as well as the colour.

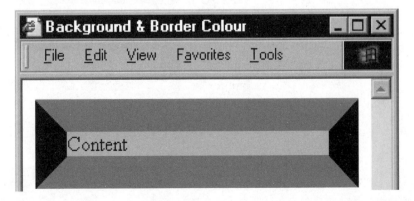

Border Style

The style for all four borders around a content box may be set collectively with the style sheet "border-style" property.

Or individually they can be specified with the properties "border-style-top", "border-style-bottom", "border-style-left" and "border-style-right".

The illustration below shows the available border styles and how each border style might be displayed by the browser:

In order to hide a border set its style property to "none".

Remember to set a width and colour as well as the style.

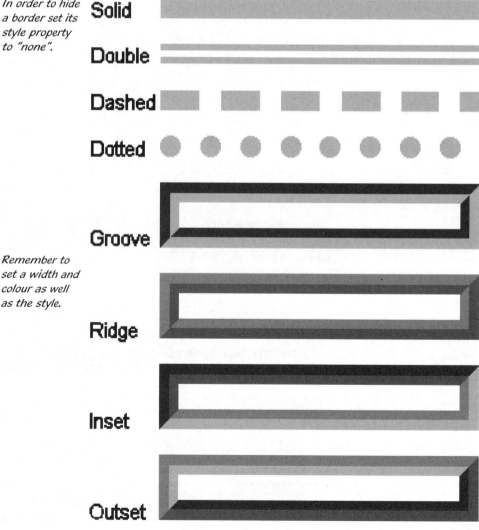

Solid

Double

Dashed

Dotted

Groove

Ridge

Inset

Outset

Border Width

The width of all four borders around a content box may be set collectively with the style sheet "border-width" property.

Or individually they can be specified with the properties "border-width-top", "border-width-bottom", "border-width-left" and "border-width-right".

The example below sets a uniform width for the silver border around the first paragraph drawn in a "double" style.

Individual border widths are specified for the black border round the second paragraph which also has a "double" style:

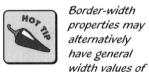

Border-width properties may alternatively have general width values of "thin", "medium" or "thick".

```
<head> <title>Border Width</title>
<style type="text/css">
<!--
#p1 {border-color:silver; border-style:double;
     border-width:10px; }
#p2 {border-color:black; border-style:double;
     border-width:10px;
     border-top-width:3px; border-bottom-width:20px; }
//-->
</style>
</head>
<body>
<p id="p1">Content</p><p id="p2">Content</p>
</body>
```

Remember to set a colour and style as well as the width.

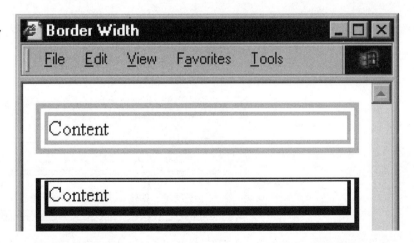

Border Shorthand

A single style sheet property called "border" may alternatively specify all the required rules to set a border.

This shorthand version can only be used when all four borders in a content box are to have the same appearance.

The "border" property collectively specifies values for a border's width, style and color with the following syntax:

```
border: [border-width] [border-style] [border-color] ;
```

In the example below the border around the first content box is set with individual properties.

The second content box border appears identical to the first one but is set using the shorthand "border" version:

The order in which the three shorthand border properties are listed is unimportant.

```
<head> <title>Border Shorthand</title>
<style type="text/css">
<!--
#s1 {border-width:5px; border-style:double;
        border-color:black; padding:5px;}
#s2 {border:5px double black; padding:5px; }
//-->
</style>
</head>

<body>
<p> <span id="s1">Content</span>
        <span id="s2">More Content</span> </p>
</body>
```

Add Padding

The padding area around the actual content in a content box can be specified with a "padding" style sheet property.

This sets a general padding width surrounding the contained content at top, bottom, left and right.

Individual padding widths can be set with "padding-top", "padding-bottom", "padding-left" and "padding-right".

This example applies overall padding in the first paragraph and top padding over the content in the second paragraph:

The HTML 4 specification requires that the "px" suffix should always follow the numeric value when assigning pixel sizes.

```
<head> <title>Padding</title>
<style type="text/css">
<!--
p {border-color:black; border-width:thin;
   border-style:solid; background color:silver;}
#p1 {padding:20px;}
#p2 {padding-top:40px;}
//-->
</style>
</head>
<body>
<p id="p1">Content</p> <p id="p2">Content</p>
</body>
```

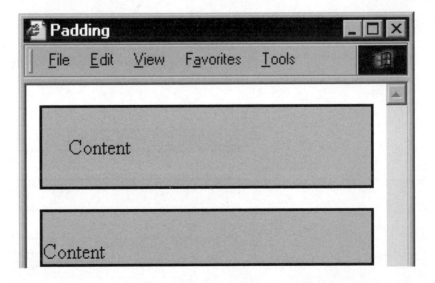

Relative Padding

Padding areas in a content box can alternatively be specified relative to other aspects of the document.

They may be specified as a percentage of the block in which they are contained or relative to the current size of font.

This example applies padding twice the width of the current font then 60% of the surrounding <div> element:

The "em" suffix is a unit value equivalent to the size of the current font.

```
<head> <title>Relative Padding</title>
<style type="text/css">
<!--
div {width:100%;}
p {border-color:black; border-width:thin;
   border-style:solid; padding-left:2em;
    background-color:silver;}
#p1 {font-size:8pt;}
#p2 {font-size:14pt;}
#p3 {padding-left:60%;}
//-->
</style>
</head>
<body> <div> <p id="p1">Content</p>
         <p id="p2">Content</p>
         <p id="p3">Content</p> </div>
</body>
```

Percentages are not relative to the content box itself but to the block that contains the content box.

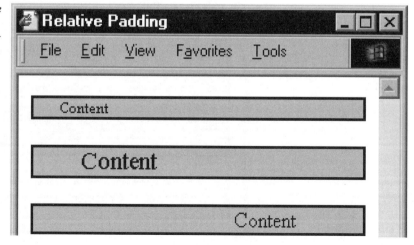

Padding Shorthand

A single style sheet property called "padding" may alternatively specify all the padding areas of a content box.

The "padding" property may collectively specify values for top, right, bottom and left padding areas.

If only one value is specified it applies to all four sides.

If two values are specified the first applies to top and bottom sides and the second applies to left and right sides.

If three values are specified the first applies to the top side, the second applies to both left and right sides and the third applies to the bottom side.

If four values are specified they apply, in sequence, to the padding areas on the top, right, bottom and left sides.

In this example the "border" shorthand property creates borders and the "padding" shorthand property adds padding:

Padding rules will be added in order to the top, right, bottom and left padding areas.

```
<head> <title>Padding Shorthand</title>
<style type="text/css">
<!--
span {border:double black 5px;}
// paddings - top right bottom left
#s1 {padding: 5px 20px 10px 100px}
//-->
</style>
</head>

<body> <p> <span id="s1">Content</span>
<span id="s2">Content</span> </p> </body>
```

Set Margins

Margin areas may be specified with the "margin" style sheet property that sets all block margins to the assigned size.

Individual margins can be set using "margin-top", "margin-bottom", "margin-left" and "margin-right" properties.

The example below sets the default body margins to zero for a <div> element to display at the extreme top left of a page.

A nested <div> element has its top and left margins set to be 20 pixels from the edge of the containing <div> element:

Margins may be interpreted differently by each browser.

```
<head> <title>Margins</title>
<style type="text/css">
<!--
body {margin:0px;}
#d1 {background-color:gray; margin:0px;
     width:200px; height:75px; }
#d2 {background-color:silver; padding:3px;
     border-width:3px; border-style:double;
     border-color:white;
     margin-top:20px; margin-left:20px;}
//-->
</style>
</head>

<body><div id="d1">
   <div id="d2"><span>Content</span></div>
</div></body>
```

Margin Shorthand

A single style sheet property called "margin" may alternatively specify all the margin areas of a content box.

The "margin" property may collectively specify values for top, right, bottom and left margin areas.

If only one value is specified it applies to all four sides.

If two values are specified the first applies to top and bottom sides and the second applies to left and right sides.

If three values are specified the first applies to the top side, the second applies to both left and right sides and the third applies to the bottom side.

If four values are specified they apply, in sequence, to the margin areas on the top, right, bottom and left sides.

In this example the "border" shorthand property creates borders, the "padding" shorthand property adds padding and the "margin" shorthand property sets margins:

Notice that the right margin value forces the second content box away right.

```
<head> <title>Margin Shorthand</title>
<style type="text/css">
<!--
span {border:solid silver 5px;}
#s1 {padding:5px; margin:5px 70px 5px 30px;}
//-->
</style>
</head>

<body> <p> <span id="s1">Content</span>
<span id="s2">Content</span> </p> </body>
```

Putting it Together

This full example uses some of the border, margin, padding and background colour properties seen in this chapter:

```
<!DOCTYPE HTML PUBLIC "-//W3C//DTD HTML 4.01//EN"
            "http://www.w3.org/TR/html4/strict.dtd">
<head> <title>Putting It Together</title>
<style type="text/css">
<!--
body{border:ridge 30px silver; background-color:white;}
p{border:dotted 3px black; padding:10px;
 background-color:silver; margin:20px;}
//-->
</style>
</head>
<body>
<h3>Borders Are Fun...</h3>
<p>If they are used<br>in sensible moderation.</p>
</body>
```

 Notice here how Internet Explorer moves the scroll bar inside the content box border — other browsers may be different.

Positioning Content Boxes

This chapter explains the system of coordinates used to reference specific points in a HTML document. There are examples demonstrating how to precisely place document content with style sheet rules.

Covers

Chapter Twelve

XYZ Coordinates

Physical position of content in a display window can be referred to using coordinates called "X", "Y" and "Z".

The X coordinate specifies the distance in pixels from the extreme left edge of the window.

The Y coordinate specifies the distance in pixels from the extreme top edge of the window.

The Z coordinate specifies the stacked position by index number of layers above the bottom window level:

To differentiate the coordinates remember that "a cross (X) means across".

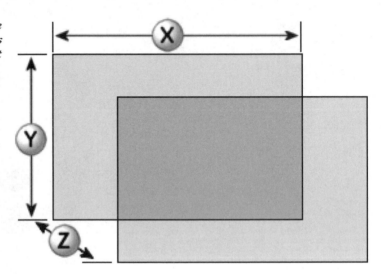

The X coordinate at the left edge of the window is zero and the Y coordinate at the top edge of the window is also zero.

A position where X=50 and Y=30 would pinpoint a location 50 pixels from the left edge and 30 pixels from the top edge.

The Z coordinate of the bottom window level has an index value of zero. Layers may be placed over this level, like transparent sheets, and are given unique Z-index values.

A window may have many layers but the top layer will always have the highest Z-index value. Each successive layer below that will have a decreasingly lower Z-index value.

Absolute Positioning

The position of document content boxes can be controlled with a style property called "position".

To determine a precise location the "position" property should be set as "absolute".

The Y coordinate of the content box is then specified by assigning a pixel value to a style property called "top". This sets the top edge of the content box at the given distance from the top of the window, or outer containing block.

Similarly the X coordinate of the content box is specified by assigning a pixel value to a style property called "left". This sets the left edge of the content block at the given distance from the top of the window, or outer containing block.

This example absolutely positions three content boxes:

If the content box is nested in a containing block the "top" and "left" positions will be set relative to that block's edges – not to those of the entire window.

```
<head> <title>Absolute Positioning</title>
<style type="text/css">
<!--
div {background-color:black; color:white; width:100px;}
#d1 {position:absolute; top:0px; left:0px; width:auto;}
#d2 {position:absolute; top:30px; left:80px;}
#d3 {position:absolute; top:10px; left:170px;}
//-->
</style>
</head>
<body> <div id="d1"><p>X=0, Y=0</p></div>
    <div id="d2"><p>X=80, Y=30</p></div>
    <div id="d3"><p>X=170, Y=10</p></div> </body>
```

Z-Order

Absolute positioning is used to specify the Z-axis stacking order of layers, in addition to setting X and Y coordinates.

The Z-index value is assigned to a style property that is called "z-index" in order to set the layers stacking position.

Layers are positioned in ascending order according to their z-index value so that higher layers can overlap those below.

This example sets some general styles for the <div> content blocks then positions them absolutely and stacked:

Number layers in increments of 10 – so it's easy to slip other layers in between later if needed.

```
<head> <title>Z-Order Positioning</title>
<style type="text/css">
<!--
div {border:solid 3px black; width:100px; height:50;
     background-color:silver; padding:3px;}
#d1 {position:absolute; top:10px; left:40px;
     z-index:10;}
#d2 {position:absolute; top:50px; left:120px;
     z-index:20;}
//-->
</style>
</head>
<body>
<div id="d1"><p>Layer 1<br>Z-Index=10</p></div>
<div id="d2"><p>Layer 2<br>Z-Index=20</p></div>
</body>
```

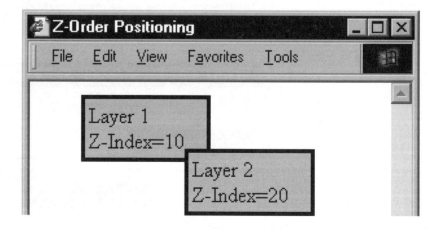

Relative Positioning

The style "position" property can be set to "relative" to adjust the position of content boxes relative to the normal flow of other content.

Regular content flow initially lays out the content box position then this can be adjusted by a style "position" rule.

In the example below all content boxes are initially laid out in the regular flow that is indicated by a dotted line.

Style rules then adjust the position of two of the content boxes relative to their regular flow position:

It is convenient to create a class to specify a relative style position rule.

```
<head><title>Relative Positioning</title>
<style type="text/css">
<!--
span {width:20; height:20; background-color:black;
      color:white; margin:5px;}
.up {position:relative; top:-15px;}
.dn {position:relative; top:15px; }
//-->
</style>
</head>
<body><p>
<span>1</span><span>2</span><span class="up">3</span>
<span>4</span><span>5</span><span class="dn">6</span>
<span>7</span><span>8</span></p>
</body>
```

Floating Boxes

A content box can be made to the extreme left or right of the current line with the style "float" property.

This property can be set to "left" or "right" to move the position of the content box.

Most importantly this allows other content to then flow around that content box.

The example below has a paragraph containing two text sentences plus an image content box that is floated to the left of the current line:

 The text wrapping may appear differently on other browsers.

```
<head><title>Floating Boxes</title>
<style type="text/css">
<!--
#i1 {float:left;}
//-->
</style>
</head>
<body>
<p>
The <img id="i1" src="lilguy.gif" width="58" height="48"
alt="lilguy">text in this paragraph simply wraps around
the floating box. After the bottom of the floating box
the lines once again start at their normal position.
</p>
</body>
```

Clear Side

Content can be prevented from wrapping around a floating box with the style "clear" property.

This can specify that its "left" or "right" side must remain clear and cannot be adjacent to a floating box.

With the example on the facing page the second sentence can be prevented from wrapping around the image content box.

The example below adds a "clear" style rule to the second sentence ensuring that it appears below the image content box rather than wrapped around it:

Content boxes floated "right" would still wrap text that has a "clear:left" side.

```
<head><title>Clear Side</title>
<style type="text/css">
<!--
#i1 {float:left;} #s1 {clear:left;}
//-->
</style>
</head>
<body>
<p>The <img id="i1" src="lilguy.gif" width="58"
height="48" alt="Lilguy">
text in this sentence wraps around the floating box.
<span id="s1">The text in the second sentence is not
allowed to wrap.</span> </p>
</body>
```

Content Box Resize

The width and height of a content box is specified with the style "width" and "height" properties.

Despite this explicit sizing instruction some browsers will automatically resize the height of the content box if the contained content will not fit the specified height.

This example shows how overflowing content may appear:

Overflow can be created when a browser uses a large font – see chapter 13 for how to control the font size.

```
<head><title>Content Box Resize</title>
<style type="text/css">
<!--
div {border:solid 1px black; margin:5px;
     width:150px; height:20px;}
//-->
</style>
</head>
<body> <div>150x20 Pixels</div>
<div>This text will not fit in a box of 150x20 pixels
</div> </body>
```

Overflow

The style "overflow" property can be used to specify how the browser should handle content that will not fit inside the content box fixed width and fixed height.

Assigning this property a "visible" value allows the browser to display the overflow content outside the content box.

Alternatively the "overflow" can be set to "hidden" which will hide any content that will not fit into the content box.

This may make it inaccessible to the user though.

A "scroll" value can be assigned to "overflow" to indicate that the content may overflow and browsers that support content box scrollbars should display them in that box.

Scroll bars handle the overflowing content in this example:

Allow extra space for the scroll bar dimensions when setting the overall content box size.

```
<head><title>Handling Overflow</title>
<style type="text/css">
<!--
div {border:solid 1px black; width:150px; height:65px;
    overflow:scroll;}
//-->
</style>
</head>
<body>
<div>This text will not fit in a box of 150x20 pixels
but the user can scroll down to read it all.</div>
</body>
```

Clipping Overflow

The style "clip" property defines a "clipping region" that will be the only visible part of a content box.

The clipping region is rectangular and is set with this syntax:

```
clip: [top] [right] [bottom] [left];
```

The parameters specify the extreme edges of the clipping region in pixel distances across the content box.

In the example below both content boxes contain the same image but the one on the right has been clipped:

Other valid measures of distance are "em" units, inches ("in") and centimetres ("cm").

```
<head><title>Clipping</title>
<style type="text/css">
<!--
body {background:gray;}
#d1 {position:absolute; top:15px; left:140px;
     clip:rect(0px 100px 80px 20px);}
//-->
</style> </head>
<body><div>
<img src="abe.gif" width="120" height="100" alt="Abe">
</div><div id="d1">
<img src="abe.gif" width="120" height="100" alt="Abe">
</div> </body>
```

Stylish Text

This chapter explores the presentation of text content in a HTML document. There are examples illustrating how to influence the manner of textual display with style rules.

Covers

Chapter Thirteen

Font Families

The style "font-family" property allows the HTML document to suggest a generic font to the browser.

This overcomes the problem that not all systems can have all fonts and so the generic family will select the most appropriate font that is available on that system.

Valid generic family names are "serif", "sans-serif", "cursive", "fantasy" and "monospace".

The "font-family" property can also suggest a list of fonts by name in a comma-delimited list.

Browsers will search for each font in turn. A generic family name should always be suggested as the last alternative in case none of the named fonts are found.

Both "cursive" and "fantasy" font families are decorative while the others are plainer, as seen in this example:

Fonts that are members of the "cursive" family usually have characters that appear as handwritten.

```
<head> <title>Font Families</title> </head>
<body> <p>
<span style="font-family:serif">Serif - </span>
<span style="font-family:sans-serif">Sans-Serif -</span>
<span style="font-family:monospace">Monospace</span><br>
<span style="font-family:cursive">Cursive - </span>
<span style="font-family:fantasy">Fantasy</span><br>
<span style="font-family:impact,modern,cursive">
          Impact,Modern or Generic Cursive</span>
</p> </body>
```

Font Size

The size of font to be used by the browser can be specified with the "font-size" style property.

Valid values may be either an exact point-size or a size relative to the surrounding font size currently in use.

Exact size is set with the suffix "pt", so 12-point is "12pt".

Relative font-size can be specified as "larger" or "smaller".

Alternatively this may be a percentage relative to the surrounding font size. For instance "font-size:200" should set the font size at double that of the surrounding font.

The following example sets a general font size for the paragraph then adds some specific "font-size" rules illustrating each of the methods given above:

Set fonts to a specific size in order to avoid overflow from content boxes.

```
<head><title>Font Size</title>
<style type="text/css">
<!--
p {font-size:12pt;} #s1 {font-size:20pt;}
    #s2 {font-size:70%;} #s3 {font-size:larger;}
//-->
</style>
</head>
<body> <p>This is a 12-point font size<br>
but <span id="s1">this is a 20-point font.</span>
<br>SIZE CAN BE <span id="s2">REDUCED</span>
OR <span id="s3">ENLARGED</span></p>   </body>
```

Font Style

The appearance of a font can be specified with the property named "font-style" to select upright or slanting characters.

If unspecified the default font style is to upright characters.

Setting the "font-style" property to "italic" will display the text in an italicised font with slanting characters.

A font style of "oblique" will also generally display as italics.

If the general font style in use is italicised the "font-style" property can specify "normal" to display upright text.

This example illustrates "normal" and "italic" font styles:

An "oblique" font style may electronically generate an italic font by slanting a normal font.

```
<head><title>Font Style</title>
<style type="text/css">
<!--
#s1 {font-style:italic;} #s2 {font-style:normal;}
#p2 {font-style:italic;}
//-->
</style>
</head>
<body><p id="p1">This paragraph uses default styling but
<span id="s1">italic style</span> can be applied.</p>
<p id="p2">This paragraph uses italic styling but
<span id="s2"> normal style</span> can be applied.</p>
</body>
```

Font Weight

The preferred boldness of text can be set with the style "font-weight" property.

Simply assigning a value of "bold" will display the text in a bold font.

Alternatively the specifications allow for the weight to be specified numerically. This numeric range starts at 100 for lightest and goes up to the boldest at 900, by steps of 100.

Normally weighted text is around 500 in the range.

The example below sets a piece of bold text then illustrates the effect of adding font weight from normal to boldest:

Setting lighter font-weights of below 500 seldom changes the appearance.

```
<head><title>Font Weight</title>
<style type="text/css">
<!--
.heavy {font-weight:bold;}
#s5 {font-weight:500;} #s6 {font-weight:600;}
#s7 {font-weight:700;} #s8 {font-weight:800;}
#s9 {font-weight:900;} p {font-size:20pt;}
//-->
</style>
</head>
<body> <p>Here is some <span class="heavy">bold</span>
text.<br>
<span id="s5"> 500</span><span id="s6"> 600</span>
<span id="s7"> 700</span><span id="s8"> 800</span>
<span id="s9"> 900</span> </p> </body>
```

Font Variant

The style "font-variant" property may be used to display text content in small capitals.

When assigned a value of "small-caps" the property suggests that the browser should attempt to capitalise the text in a smaller font than the one in current use.

The example below illustrates the results of specifying a "font-variant" of "small-caps" in three different browsers:

```
<head><title>Font Variant</title>
<style type="text/css">
<!--
p {font-size:16pt;}
span{font-variant:small-caps;}
//-->
</style></head>
<body>
<p>The <span>small caps</span> font variant.</p>
</body>
```

Some browsers may just capitalise the text for this style property – as seen in this example with Internet Explorer (the middle illustration).

Line Height

The style "line-height" property can specify line spacing.

The height can be specified either as a font point size or as a percentage of the font size in general use by the text. For instance, with a font-size of 12pt setting the line height at 300% would create a line spacing of 36pt.

In the example below the general font size is 12pt and the "line-height" is set at 36pt. Consequently the browser will add extra space over each line of general text.

When the larger 36pt text is encountered an equivalent amount of extra space is added over it and the entire line:

When text has more than one font size the browser will calculate a line height from the tallest font.

```
<head><title>Line Height</title>
<style type="text/css">
<!--
p {font-size:12pt;line-height:300%;}
span {font-size:36pt;}
//-->
</style> </head>
<body> <p>General font size in this paragraph is 12pt.
<br>But here is some<span> 36pt </span> text.<br>
All line heights are also specified as 36pt.</p> </body>
```

Font Shorthand

All the font style properties described earlier in this chapter can be specified together with the "font" property.

Each required property is specified in a list like this:

```
font: style variant weight size family;
```

Any of the properties above may be omitted from the list but any included should appear in the given sequential order.

The example below uses the "font" shorthand property to apply font style rules to a tag, an id and a class:

Specific fonts must still be set with the "font-family" property.

```
<head><title>Font Shorthand</title>
<style type="text/css">
<!--
p {font:12pt serif;}
#s1 {font:bold 28pt;}
span.doric {font:italic bold 16pt;}
//-->
</style>
</head>
<body> <p>The main attraction of Gortys is the
<br><span id="s1">Code of Laws</span>
<br>These were carved on massive blocks of stone by the
<span class="doric">Dorians</span> </p> </body>
```

Some browsers may not support font shorthand – it is safer to set individual font properties.

Text and Content Alignment

The style "text-align" property is used to align text in a content box as either "left", "right" or "center".

It usefully also aligns any other content such as images.

The example below aligns text in three <div> content boxes together and illustrates a centred image:

The "text-align" style property is used with "center" to replace the old HTML <center> tag.

```
<head><title>Text Align</title>
<style type="text/css">
<!--
div {border:1px solid silver; padding:5px; margin:5px;}
#d1 {text-align:left;}
#d2 {text-align:right;}
#d3 {text-align:center;}
//-->
</style>
</head>
<body>
<div id="d1">text-align is "left"</div>
<div id="d2">text-align is "right"</div>
<div id="d3">text-align is "center"<br>
<img src="g.gif" width="29" height="24" alt="Guy"></div>
</body>
```

Text Decoration

The style "text-decoration" property may add features to text with "underline", "overline" and "line-through" values.

It may also specify "blink" to flash text but this may not be supported in all browsers.

Blinking text can be extremely annoying and is best avoided.

In this example the "text-decoration" properties create text with underlines, overlines and strike through:

Text decoration "underline" is used in place of the old HTML <u> tag.

```
<head><title>Text Decoration</title>
<style type="text/css">
<!--
div {border:1px solid silver; padding:5px; margin:5px;}
#d1 {text-decoration:underline;}
#d2 {text-decoration:line-through;}
#d3 {text-decoration:overline;}
//-->
</style>
</head>
<body>
<div id="d1">This is underlined text.</div>
<div id="d2">This text has a line through.</div>
<div id="d3">This text is overlined.</div>
</body>
```

Text decoration "line-through" is used in place of old HTML <strike> tags.

Indenting Text

Traditionally paragraphs have their first line of text indented in order to make the overall flow of text more acceptable.

In HTML the style "text-indent" property can specify the amount to indent the first line of text in a content block.

The value may be either a fixed amount, like 10 pixels, or a percentage of the width of the containing box.

This example uses the "em" font size units to specify how much the start of each paragraph should be indented:

Specify a negative value to "outdent" the first line of content blocks.

```
<head><title>Text Indent</title>
<style type="text/css">
<!--
p {text-indent:2em; }
//-->
</style>
</head>
<body>
<p>One of the best adventures of Crete is a visit to the
Gorge of Samaria.</p>
<p>It is reputed to be the longest gorge in Europe and
may take anywhere between four to seven hours to walk
through.</p>
</body>
```

Letter Spacing

Extra space can be added between each character with the style "letter-spacing" property.

The property can specify a length that is to be added to the normal text spacing between characters.

This may be a fixed distance expressed as pixels like "10px".

Alternatively the extra space can be expressed as a distance relative to the font size by using an "em" unit like "1em".

In the example below the first <span> adds extra spacing of "1em" and the second <span> adds extra spacing of "10px":

Use "em" units in preference to pixels to display the text spacing appropriate to the text size.

```
<!DOCTYPE HTML PUBLIC "-//W3C//DTD HTML 4.01//EN"
                  "http://www.w3.org/TR/html4/strict.dtd">
<head><title>Letter Spacing</title>
<style type="text/css">
<!--
p {font-size:20pt;}
#s1 {letter-spacing:1em; }
#s2 {letter-spacing:10px; }
//-->
</style>
</head>

<body>
<p>Added <span id="s1">SPACE</span><br>
and <span id="s2">MORE</span> space.</p>
</body>
```

Word Spacing

Spaces can be added to the normal spacing between words of text with the style "word-spacing" property.

This works like the "letter-spacing" property shown on the facing page but may not be implemented in all browsers.

This example adds a value of "1em" to the default spacing:

```
<head><title>Word Spacing</title>
<style type="text/css">
<!--
p {font-size:14pt;}
span {word-spacing:1em; }
//-->
</style>
</head>
<body>
<p>This is <span>spaced out</span> text.</p>
</body>
```

Notice that Internet Explorer (the middle illustration) has not actually implemented extra word spacing here.

Text Direction

The direction of text flow can be controlled with the HTML 4 <bdo> </bdo> tags.

Its "dir" attribute can specify "ltr" for normal left-to-right direction or "rtl" for right-to-left text direction.

This is useful with languages that run right-to-left where it is advisable for the whole text block to be contained in <pre> </pre> tags to conserve spacing and line breaks.

Languages are specified with the "lang" attribute which recognises special two letter codes for each language.

Two-letter codes include "en" (English), "fr" (French), "de" (German), "it" (Italian), "nl" (Dutch), "es" (Spanish), "el" (Greek), "pt" (Portugese), "ar" (Arabic), "he" Hebrew, "ru" Russian, "zh" (Chinese), "ja" (Japanese) and "hi" (Hindi).

This example displays Hebrew text correctly as right-to-left:

The examples on these two pages need the HebrewUniversal font installed.

```
<head>
<meta http-equiv="Content-Language" content="en">
<meta http-equiv="Content-Type"
      content="text/html; charset=utf-8">
<title>BiDirectional Order</title>
<style type="text/css">
<!--
bdo {font-family: HebrewUniversal; font-size:20pt;}
//-->
</style> </head>
<body> <pre>
Hello and<bdo dir="rtl" lang="he" id="bdo2"> שלום </bdo>
from Israel.</pre> </body>
```

Right-To-Left Style

The text direction in a browser is normally left-to-right but can be changed with the style "unicode-bidi" property.

Setting this to "override" will allow the direction to be determined by the style "direction" as "rtl" or "ltr".

This starts the entire text content at the right-hand side of the display area and is more suitable for larger sections of text in languages written right-to-left.

In the example below the normal text direction is changed to right-to-left for the entire second paragraph:

Use <bdo> for right-to-left text inserted in a left-to-right text paragraph.

```
<head>
<meta http-equiv="Content-Language" content="en">
<meta http-equiv="Content-Type"
      content="text/html; charset=utf-8">
<title>Unicode BiDirection Override</title>
<style type="text/css">
<!--
#s1 {font-family: cursive; font-size: 12pt; }
#s2 {unicode-bidi:override; direction: rtl;
     font-family:HebrewUniversal; font-size:20pt;}
//-->
</style>
</head>
<body>
<p id="s1">Happy New Year</p>
<p id="s2" lang="he">שנה טובה</p>
</body>
```

Text Capitalisation

The style "text-transform" property can be used to convert the capitalisation of text content.

It may be used to transform text into "uppercase" or "lowercase" or it may make the first letter of each word into a capital letter when set as "capitalize".

This example illustrates each type of transformation:

Text may not be transformed for content in languages that use other than standard Latin characters.

```
<head><title>Text Transform</title>
<style type="text/css">
<!--
div {border:1px solid silver; padding:5px; margin:5px;}
#d1 {text-transform:uppercase;}
#d2 {text-transform:lowercase;}
#d3 {text-transform:capitalize;}
//-->
</style>
</head>
<body>
<div id="d1">This Line is Transformed to Uppercase</div>
<div id="d2">This Line is Transformed to Lowercase</div>
<div id="d3">This Line is Transformed to Capitalize
</div>
</body>
```

List and Table Styles

This chapter presents further options for how text lists and content tables may be displayed in a HTML document. There are examples illustrating how their presentation can be influenced with Cascading Style Sheet rules.

Covers

Chapter Fourteen

List Style Types

The list styles available in HTML 4 can alternatively be specified by the style "list-style-type" property.

This may specify that each list item should be marked as "disc", "circle", "square", "decimal", "lower-roman", "upper-roman", "lower-alpha", or "upper-alpha".

The specifications also allow for foreign language list styles to be marked as "hebrew", "georgian", "armenian", "katakana", "cjk-ideographic" or "hiragana".

In the event that the specified list style type is not supported the browser will default to the "decimal" numbering style.

With alpha marking most browsers will list the first 26 items with successive lettering then start with "AA", "BB", etc.

The example below illustrates a simple list specifying the "disc" type of list style to create filled circular bullet points:

 Browsers may not support foreign language list style types.

```
<head><title>List Style Type</title>
<style type="text/css">
<!--
ol { list-style-type: disc; }
//-->
</style>
</head>
<body>
<ol> <li>Pascal Programming</li>
     <li>Java Programming</li>
</ol>
</body>
```

List Style Position

The position of item markers in a list can be set with the style "list-style-position" property.

This allows the marker to be either "outside" or "inside" the content box containing the list, as seen in this example:

Notice that the first style rule sets the marker type for both unordered lists.

```
<head><title>List Style Position</title>
<style type="text/css">
<!--
ul {list-style-type:circle; }
#list1 { list-style-position: outside; }
#list2 { list-style-position: inside; }
//-->
</style> </head>

<body>
<ul id="list1"><li>Pascal<br>Programming With Units</li>
        <li>Java<br>Programming With Classes</li></ul>
<ul id="list2"><li>Pascal<br>Programming With Units</li>
        <li>Java<br>Programming With Classes</li> </ul>
</body>
```

List Style Image

More creative lists can be made by replacing the standard markers for each item with a custom marker image.

The location of the image to be used should be specified with the style "list-style-image" property.

It must be assigned inside brackets following the term "url".

The location can be either an absolute address, such as "http://domain/pic.gif", or a relative address like "pic.gif".

If the image is unavailable the list uses "decimal" markers.

In the example below the list markers are set as an image with a relative location address in a style-sheet class:

Remember to surround the location address with quotes.

```
<head><title>List Style Image</title>
<style type="text/css">
<!--
ol.lilguy { list-style-image: url("lilguy.gif"); }
//-->
</style>
</head>
<body>
<ol class="lilguy">
  <li>Pascal<br>Programming With Units</li>
  <li>Java<br>Programming With Classes</li> </ol>
</body>
```

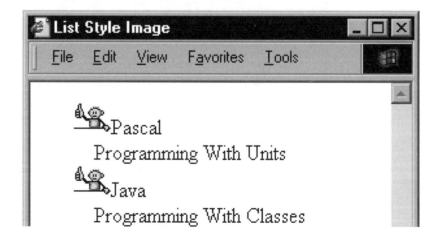

List Style Shorthand

All list styles can be specified together using the "list-style" property to set the list's type, position and marker image.

The example below uses this shorthand method to specify the list properties for an outer list and a nested list:

Notice with the outer list that the marker will display as the specified type if the image cannot be found.

```
<head><title>List Style Shorthand</title>
<style type="text/css">
<!--
#outerlist {list-style: square inside url{"star.gif"}; }
#innerlist {list-style: disc outside url("duke.gif");}
//-->
</style> </head>
<body>
<ul id="outerlist">
  <li>Pascal<br>Programming With Units</li>
  <li>Java<br>Programming With Classes</li>
  <li><ul id="innerlist">
    <li>Applets</li>
    <li>Swing Interface</li>
  </ul></li>
</ul> </body>
```

Table Caption Side

The position of a table caption relative to the table may be specified with the style "caption-side" property.

This can set the caption's position at the "top", "bottom", "left" or "right" of the table.

In the example below the "caption-side" property positions the caption to the right of the table.

The caption is 80 pixels wide, with a left margin of 5 pixels, and is vertically aligned with the bottom of the table:

The property "vertical-align" can specify "top", "middle" or "bottom".

```
<head> <title>Caption Side</title>
<style type="text/css">
<!--
caption { caption-side:right; margin-left:5px;
          width:80px; vertical-align:bottom;
          color:white; background-color:black;
          font-weight:bold;}
//-->
</style> </head>
<body>
<p> <table width="150px"
          cellspacing="3" border="1">
<caption>Descriptive Caption</caption>
<tr><td>1</td><td>2</td><td>3</td></tr>
<tr><td>4</td><td>5</td><td>6</td></tr>
</table> </p>
</body>
```

Browsers that do not support this property will normally position the caption above the table.

Collapsing Table Borders

Individual table border styles can be applied to cells, rows and columns with their style "border" property as usual.

Visually this can appear cluttered but the "border-collapse" style property can be set to "collapse" so that only the most prominent border will be displayed.

The example below specifies a single-pixel silver border around each cell but these are collapsed to unite together:

The overall table border has prominence over other table border styles.

```
<head> <title>Border-Collapse</title>
<style type="text/css">
<!--
table { border-collapse: collapse;
        border: 5px double silver;}
  td  { border: 1px solid silver; padding:1em;}
  td.dash  { border: 5px dashed black; }
  td.solid { border: 5px solid gray; }
//-->
</style>
<body> <table>
<tr> <td>1</td><td>2</td><td>3</td> </tr>
<tr> <td class="dash">4</td><td>5</td>
     <td class="solid">6</td> </tr>
</table> </body>
```

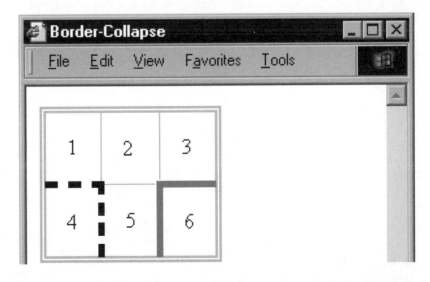

Empty Cell Borders

Table cells that contain no content may have their borders hidden by setting the style "empty-cell" property to "hide".

This property can be applied to the entire table so that all empty cell borders are hidden.

Note that an empty cell's background will remain visible even when the "empty-cell" property is set to "hide".

The example below hides the borders of all its empty cells.

In order to make cell 4 completely invisible its background colour is set to match the page background:

If this table had a background colour, that would still be visible overall.

```
<head> <title>Empty Cells</title>
<style type="text/css">
<!--
table { text-align:center;}
td { border:black 5px double; background-color:silver;}
#cell4 { background-color:white; }
//-->
</style>
<body> <p>
<table width="150px" cellspacing="3">
<tr><td>1</td><td>2</td><td></td></tr>
<tr><td id="cell4"></td><td>5</td><td>6</td></tr>
</table> </p> </body>
```

Styling Backgrounds

This chapter demonstrates how style sheet techniques may display content backgrounds in a HTML document. Further style rule examples illustrate cursor choice, content clipping and automatic content insertion.

Covers

Chapter Fifteen

Background Colour

The background colour of HTML 4 elements can be specified with the style "background-color" property.

Foreground colour is normally black by default but can be changed for each element with the style "color" property.

This example illustrates how background and foreground colours may be specified for different elements:

It is sometimes useful to set a background colour to be "transparent".

```
<head><title>Background &amp; Foreground Colour</title>
<style type="text/css">
<!--
body {background-color:white; }
h3 { background-color: black; color:white; }
p  { background-color: silver; }
//-->
</style> </head>
<body> <h3>Hiking</h3> <p>Both Heraklion and Chania have
clubs that organize hiking trips.</p>
<h3>Flora</h3> <p>Crete is a year-round showcase of
flowers and trees.</p> </body>
```

Background Image

The background of a HTML 4 element can feature an image using the style "background-image" property.

This states the location of an image as an absolute or relative address between brackets and preceded by the term "url" .

A background colour should also be specified that will display beneath the image.

The specified background colour will be displayed even when the image is not available and the colour will show through any transparent areas of the background image.

Browsers will normally "tile" the image by repeating it both horizontally and vertically across the element background.

This example tiles an image over the document body background and on top of a white background colour:

Remember to surround the image address with quotes.

```
<head> <title>Background Image</title>
<style type="text/css">
<!--
body {background-color:white; text-align:center;
      background-image: url("mug.gif"); }
p {font-size:36pt; font-style:italic; font-weight:bold;}
//-->
</style> </head> <body> <p>Coffee<br>Time !</p> </body>
```

Background Repeat

The way a background image is repeated across an element can be set with the style "background-repeat" property.

If a "repeat-x" value is specified the image will be repeated in a single horizontal line only.

If a "repeat-y" value is specified the image will be repeated in a single vertical line only.

In both cases the sequence starts with the top left corner of the image at the top left corner of the element (x=0, y=0).

This example creates two <div> content blocks illustrating horizontally and vertically repeated background images:

This example is repeating this single image:

```
<head><title>Background Repeat</title>
<style type="text/css">
<!--
body {text-align:center; color:white; font-weight:bold;}
div {position:absolute;top:20px;width:200px;height:60px;
background-image:url("box.gif");background-color:black;}
#d1 { background-repeat: repeat-x; left:20px;}
#d2 { background-repeat: repeat-y; left:140px;}
//-->
</style> </head>
<body>
<div id="d1"><br>repeat-x</div>
<div id="d2"><br>repeat-y</div>
</body>
```

Use "no-repeat" to stop the background image from repeating.

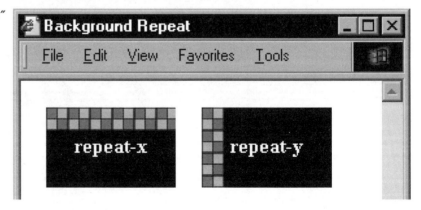

Background Position

The position of a background image can be specified using the style "background-position" property to set its top left corner relative to the edges of its containing content box.

Position values may be expressed as pixels or percentages or with keywords "top", "bottom", "left", "right" and "center".

Keywords cannot be mixed with pixel or percentage values.

If only one length value is specified it will set the horizontal position of the background image.

If two length values are specified the first sets the horizontal position while the second will set the vertical position.

The following example demonstrates the use of keywords and percentages to set the background image positions:

The "center" keyword used alone centres the background image on both horizontal and vertical axes.

```
<head><title>Background Position</title>
<style type="text/css">
<!--
div {position:absolute;top:5px;width:100px;height:60px;
background-image:url("box.gif");background-color:silver}
#d1 { background-position:center;
      background-repeat:no-repeat; left:20px;}
#d2 { background-position: 50% 100%;
      background-repeat:no-repeat; left:140px;}
//-->
</style> </head>
<body> <div id="d1">center</div>
       <div id="d2">50% 100%</div> </body>
```

The position of "50% 100%" is equivalent to the same position with keywords "center bottom".

Background Attachment

Typically background images will scroll along with the document but they can be fixed using the style property called "background-attachment".

Setting this property to "fixed" keeps the background image position constant when the rest of the document scrolls.

This example fixes a horizontally repeated image at a specified distance from the top of the window:

This is useful to ensure that background logos are always visible.

```
<head> <title>Background Attachment</title>
<style type="text/css">
<!--
body { background-attachment:fixed; text-align:center;
 background-position:0% 10%; background-repeat:repeat-x;
  background-image:url("box.gif"); }
//-->
</style>
</head> <body> <h1>Heading</h1> </body>
```

Background Shorthand

All the background properties can be set together using the style "background" property with this syntax:

```
background: colour image repeat position attachment ;
```

Some or all of the above may be specified, and in any order.

The valid values are those stated on the previous pages in this chapter for "background-color", "background-image". "background-repeat", "background-position" and "background-attachment".

In the example below the <div> element background repeats a fixed image across the bottom of its content box:

 Specify font sizes to absolutely control text in content boxes.

```
<head> <title>Background Shorthand</title>
<style type="text/css">
<!--
body {text-align:center; font:14pt cursive black;}
div {width:90%; height:70px; border:3px double black;}
#d1 {
background: white url("mug.gif") bottom repeat-x fixed;}
//-->
</style>
</head>
<body>
<div id="d1">Coffee Time !</div>
</body>
```

Visibility

Content boxes may be hidden by setting the style "visibility" property to "hidden" or revealed when it is set to "visible".

This is most useful with scripts to toggle the visibility of content in response to an event triggered by the user.

The example below creates two content boxes at the same XY position but with different Z-index values.

The top layer is initially hidden but may be revealed when the user places the cursor over the third content box:

Notice how the style sheet can apply style rules to several tags at once.

```
<head><title>Visibility</title>
<style type="text/css">
<!--
#d1,#d2,#d3 {position:absolute; top:20px; left:20px;
width:100px;}
#d2 {z-index:10; visibility:hidden; background-
color:black; color:white;}
#d3 { top:40px;}
//-->
</style> </head>
<body> <div id="d1">Action is OFF</div>
       <div id="d2">Action is ON</div>
<div id="d3" onmouseover="d2.style.visibility='visible'"
            onmouseout="d2.style.visibility='hidden'">
Roll pointer over here to turn on.</div> </body>
```

The snippet of script code used here is just the version suitable with Microsoft Internet Explorer.

Cursors

The type of cursor to be displayed over elements can be specified with the style "cursor" property.

Common valid pointer values include "default", "crosshair", "move", "text", "wait", and "help" as seen in the table below:

The browser will determine the precise appearance of each cursor.

Name	Cursor	Pointer Type
default		Browsers default cursor
crosshair		Pinpoint selector
move		Selection relocator
text		Text highlighter
wait		Program busy indicator
help		Help available indicator
resize		Edge indicator
url		Specify remote cursor address

The resize cursor is a pointer that indicates a direction and can be set as "n-resize", "s-resize", "w-resize", "e-resize", "ne-resize", "nw-resize", "se-resize", or "sw-resize".

In the table above the "e-resize" cursor is illustrated.

A custom cursor can be used by specifying the location of a cursor image with the term "url":

```
cursor: url( "http://domain/folder/special.cur" );
```

The location is stated as either a relative or absolute address between quotes and inside brackets after the "url" term.

Hyperlink Colours

HTML 4 <a> tags have the following "pseudo-classes" that can be useful to influence the appearance of their content:

Name	Description
:link	The default state of an un-visited hyperlink
:hover	A hyperlink that has the cursor over it
:active	A hyperlink that is being clicked by the user
:visited	The default state of a visited hyperlink

A style sheet may set different property values for each pseudo-class to indicate the hyperlink's state to the user.

This example sets colour and font properties for each state:

Keep to one font style for all states to avoid the content "jumping" to accommodate changing styles.

```
<head><title>Link Colours</title>
<style type="text/css">
<!--
a {font-size:18pt}
a:link    {color:red; font-style:normal; }
a:hover   {color:fuchsia; font-weight:bold; }
a:active  {color:green; font-weight:bold;}
a:visited {color:blue; font-style:italic}
//-->
</style> </head>
<body> <p><a href="x.html">Link 1</a>
       <a href="y.html">Link 2</a>
       <a href="z.html">Link 3</a></p> </body>
```

Additional Content

Style sheets may automatically insert content into HTML 4 elements with the "pseudo-elements" listed in this table:

Name	Description
:before	The space immediately before element content
:after	The space immediately after element content
:first-letter	The first letter of a <p> element
:first-line	The first line of a <p> element

This example uses pseudo-elements to add three dots after every <h3> heading, emphasise the first letter of each paragraph and end each paragraph with an exclamation mark:

Pseudo-elements may not be fully implemented in all browsers.

```
<head> <title>Additional Content</title>
<style type="text/css">
<!--
p {font-family:cursive;}
h3:after {content:"...";}
p:first-letter {font-weight:bold; font-size:larger;}
p:after {content:" !";}
//-->
</style>
</head>
<body> <h3>And Finally</h3>
<p>HTML 4 is Fantastic Fun in easy steps</p>
</body>
```

What Next?

This book will, hopefully, have provided you with a great introduction to HTML 4 with Cascading Style Sheets for the creation of exciting visual content.

Catering for future browser devices, style sheets properties already exist to control aural content, as listed in this table:

Property Type	Property Names
Volume	volume
Pause	pause, pause-before, pause-after
Cue	cue, cue-before, cue-after
Mixing	play-during
Spatial	azimuth, elevation
Voice	voice, voice-family, speech, speech-rate, pitch, pitch-range, stress, richness
Speak	speak, speak-header, speak-pronunciation, speak-numeral

Longer term plans for Internet content are increasingly focusing on the Extensible Markup Language (XML).

This is like a stricter version of HTML that adds the ability to create your own tags and has other features that are well suited to data handling.

For the very latest developments in HTML and XML refer to the W3C Web site at http://www.w3c.org.

The countless millions of HTML documents that are in current existence ensure that implementation of newer specifications must be a gradual building process.

This means that HTML documents created with the strict HTML 4 standards used throughout this book will remain valid for the foreseeable future – happy coding!

Index